Becoming Aware of
Values

Second Edition

Becoming Aware of

Values

Second Edition

BERT K. SIMPSON, Ph. D.
Consultant in Valuing Education
and
Instructor in Valuing, Orange County Department of Education
Orange County, California

formerly

Associate Dean, Graduate School of Human Behavior
United States International University
San Diego, California

Director of Research
Manitoba New Start, Inc.
Manitoba, Canada

Specialist in Higher Education
Coordinating Council for Higher Education
State of California
Sacramento, California

Assistant Professor of Education
Biola College
La Mirada, California

Published by
PENNANT PRESS
A division of Progressive Playthings, Inc., San Diego, California 92120

ISBN 0-913458-10-4

Printed in the United States of America

Preface

Becoming Aware of Values is a guidebook in the uses of the *valuing* process. The methods and techniques suggested have been tried and proven in hundreds of classrooms. They work. Valuing has transformed the lives of those who have employed it and who have expanded upon it, whether they have been teachers, parents, or students.

The reader is being asked to do more than just absorb the ideas in this book. You are being asked to apply them, to test them, to see whether they work for you. Hopefully they will lead you to discover new uses for valuing, and especially to develop improvements in valuing as applied to the field of education.

I have tried to outline some of the theory and some of the methodology for valuing. Its techniques are useful to persons of all ages and of all walks of life, but it is most directly useful to those who work professionally with children.

The effects of the valuing process on adults and children has been thoroughly researched over the past 8 years and the evidence of positive change has been well documented. The evidence gathered to date on the application of valuing shows that patterns of behavior and attitude have been changed from apathy, conformity, and underachievement, to the more positive enhancing attitudes of caring, self-direction, and resourcefulness.

This book is a tool. It must be used skillfully to be effective. It is, however, only a first step in the long road of teaching and learning responsible behavior. It is only a beginning for thinking, sharing, and seeking an understanding about ourselves and others, a beginning which I hope you will develop more fully.

Wherever I have failed to make the methods clear, you become the loser. Wherever you fail to make the methods usable tools, we all become losers. I pray that you will find within the covers of this book the means to move toward greater enhancement for yourself and others, and in your recognition of the enhancements that others share toward you. I also hope that your modeling as an enhancing person will infect those that come in contact with you and that this infection will spread like an epidemic throughout your home, your school, your community and the nation.

Bert K. Simpson

Acknowledgements

Becoming Aware of Values is a natural out-growth of the ever-increasing application of the valuing process originated by Dr. Harold Lasswell of Yale University and its adaptation to the field of education by Dr. W. Ray Rucker and his associates. Although several individuals have taken the leadership in the development of methods related to this approach, it has only been within the past years that school districts have begun to develop a total curriculum based upon the valuing approach.

This second edition is an attempt to bring together within one volume a sampling of the materials available in this field. Most of the strategies were developed out of my relationship with Dr. Rucker and with those who were graduate students during my time as Associate Dean of the Graduate School of Human Behavior, U.S. International University, San Diego, California. Many of these ideas have been transformed into activities by teachers throughout California.

Special recognition must be given to the following districts for the development of outstanding curriculum guides which have included material directly related to one or more of the eight values discussed in this handbook:

Ontario-Montclair School District for their guide entitled: *Margarita Goals Project.*

Santee School District for their guide entitled: *Teaching for Responsible Behavior.*

Merced City School District for their guide entitled: *The Values Approach to Drug Education - Grades K-8.*

Coronado Unified School District for their guide entitled: *Teacher's Guides to the Coronado Plan for Drug Abuse Prevention Education — K-3 and 4-6.*

A review of the curriculum guides that have used the valuing approach will illustrate how many of the strategies in this book have been in the public domain for years. Like jokes, folk songs, and historical incidents, they continue to be passed on, adapted, and redesigned for particular needs time and again. This edition contains only a select group of the more well-known and well-used techniques.

The creation and testing of several of the more original activities were due to the dedication of a former primary level teacher, Jimmy Ann Simpson. Jimmy Ann is not only my wife and mother to our three children, but also a partner in making real the application of valuing in our home. The word search examples were a joint effort of my wife and Andrew B. Simpson, age 10, my son, and one of my most invaluable "consultants" in the development of both the suggested activities and the valuing games from the viewpoint of a participant.

Dr. Jimmy Phelps, Associate Superintendent of the Santee, California School District, provided many insights into value-oriented educational activities.

It has been my privilege over the past year to work closely with Dr. Herbert O. Brayer who provided the leadership in the original Coronado plan and is currently Coordinator of the Drug Abuse Prevention Education Center, Orange County Department of Education, Santa Ana, California. Dr. Brayer is also a consultant to various school districts, state departments of education, and other agencies throughout the country. I wish to recognize his valuable contributions and active leadership in the field of valuing.

This book would not have been possible without the special skills in both manuscript reading and typing by Ruth Spiering, Marian Caves, and Nancy Miller. A special note of thanks to the Pennant Press staff for their work in publishing.

Appreciation must also be given to Robert Sanchez, manager, and Mary Lou Rey, waitress at the Colony Kitchen Restaurant in Oceanside, California for allowing me to use a quiet booth as an "office" and "conference center" for many Fridays during the later stages of the draft.

Any errors or omissions are squarely my responsibility. I would appreciate any suggestions for corrections or for materials which may be useful for subsequent editions of this book.

Bert K. Simpson

CONTENTS

SECTION ONE

VALUING AND ITS APPLICATION

1

WHAT IS VALUING?

Valuing is a process. It is founded on a holistic framework of universal needs. It is a pattern for living.

Simply stated, valuing begins with an understanding that man has eight basic needs. These needs are *affection, respect, skill, enlightenment, influence* (or *power*), *wealth, well-being,* and *responsibility* (or *rectitude*). Although there are many different lists of basic needs, all possible needs of man can be accommodated under one or more of the above broadly-defined need areas. These eight pegs become the reference points for the framework.

Implicit in this framework is the concept that every man, regardless of his race, creed, national origin, color, or period of history, has the same eight needs. It should be remembered, however, that needs, like the weather, are always in a state of flux. The rank order of these needs is constantly changing and the needs are never satisfied for all times. Within the space of just a few hours, each of us strives for enhancement in at least half of these needs.

Why should we study about valuing? Why should anyoꞁe be interested in it? I suppose that, if you are an educator, you are looking for a new tool or technique that will help children learn and make teaching a more enjoyable lʼne of work. If so, valuing will prove to be useful. If you ɑre also a parent, valuing can strengthen your marriage and also build a stronger bond with your own children. If you are a student "of any age", valuing can assist you to determine who you are socially and psychologically, to identify the areas of your life that require modification, and even to suggest the ways in which to change. I do not mean to overstate the claims; however, I am confident in the potential of valuing to be a positive force for both individual and organizational change.

*The reader should carefully note that throughout this book we will be using the word **values** but, as indicated above, we define this as **basic needs.***

The valuing process is founded upon a holistic framework, that is, all human wants and needs are contained within one or more of these eight value categories. In fact, I would assume that it would be almost impossible in human nature to find any one of these eight categories in pure form. The manifestation of our affection for one another is in many ways dependent upon our skill. The respect that we have for ourselves is often demonstrated by our sense of well-being. The influence that we exert over others may be contingent upon our wealth or our enlightenment; our adherence to moral and ethical principles in terms of this framework, characterized by the word *responsibility* (or rectitude), is often conditioned by the degree of respect we seek from our peers.

Since the central focus of this book is the field of education, we will need to constantly relate the valuing process to the needs and wants of children. All eight of these value categories are needed by children at all grade levels and, I might add, are manifested from the cradle to the grave.

As educators, we need to be aware of these eight basic needs. Bells should ring and a red warning light should flash on and off when we see deprivations in one or more of these areas manifested by a child. These eight words are *the needs* of children. They are preeminent to anything else that we do in education. Our classrooms have many children who cry out for affection, who lack self-respect or respect for others, who have not acquired basic skills or even recognized the skills they have already obtained. In many ways, as children proceed through the grades, they perceive an increasing deprivation of influence. Decisions are made for them. They are told where to go, when to go, what to be, who to be, and how to be. The choices they are offered are limited. And little or no rationale is given for many things that occur to them. Rather than sharing more and more in the decision-making processes of education as they proceed through the school years, they sense an increasing loss of influence. Wealth, often defined only in terms of material goods, is given them rather than earned. Wealth is discussed as some goal they may achieve after school has been completed.

One of the brighter aspects of valuing in education today is physical well-being. Nurses, counselors, doctors, school psychologists, and others are constantly alert to the physical needs of school children. Required immunizations, school lunch programs, and periodic physical check-ups are normal procedures in many schools today. There is, however, another aspect of well-being that is often neglected. Questions concerning the mood and feeling in the classroom need to be raised. Are children happy? Do they like what they are learning? Do they want to be part of the learning environment? We have long recognized that well-being is an integral part of our ability to learn. How can learning take place when one is sad? How can one concentrate on subject matter when one is unhappy or depressed or angry?

Responsibility also plays a key role in the ability of education to function effectively. Why should a child study history? Is it right for him to do so? Does he understand and accept it as a right? Or does he do so because he is told to do so, because it is required? Why do we assume that children know that they should go to school? Why do we assume that is is their responsibility to be there and to learn? Why do we burden ourselves with the responsibilities of indoctrination, with supervision, with control over children who can learn to assume responsibilities for themselves, to supervise themselves, to control themselves, and to understand the rightness of education for themselves and others?

The valuing process provides a framework for helping children to acquire these value areas for themselves, thereby easing the responsibility and the burden that we have placed upon teachers. I doubt that anyone would deny the need to instill within our educational system a strong sense of affection, respect, skill, enlightenment, wealth, influence, responsibility, and well-being. This book, hopefully, will outline the processes whereby these principles can be applied and offer leads so that educators can seek other suggested strategies and techniques for application in their own classroom.

2

DIMENSIONS OF VALUING

*Valuing is a **three-dimensional** process. The first dimension is to **develop** within ourselves each one of these basic need areas. The second dimension is to **participate** in the sharing and shaping of these eight basic areas in the lives of others. And the third dimension is to **recognize** the ways in which others influence the shaping and sharing of values within ourselves.*

For example, let us take a look at the category of respect. Every child needs to develop self-respect. He needs to see himself as someone important, someone unique. There is no one like him anywhere in the world. He needs to be able to understand that "I am the only me" in the world and that he has a contribution to make that no one else can make because there is no one else in his unique position. Can he identify his good points? Can he recognize his fine qualities? Can he, in a sense, pat himself on the back? I see children every day who exhibit in words and actions that they are nobody, and that they will always be a nobody. There is nothing in themselves that they admire, nothing that they honor, and nothing that they can look up to. Self-respect, however, is only one of the three dimensions of respect that every child must learn to develop within himself.

The second dimension of respect relates to the shaping and sharing of respect toward others. Can he identify those whom he respects? Can he identify what characteristics in other people he respects, and why? The Bible says "As a man thinks in his heart, so is he."[1] A recent book was entitled *You Are What You Eat*.[2] I would add a third maxim: "We are the copy of our models."

A third and possibly the most important dimension of valuing is the recognition of those who respect us. I have long been convinced that we have an amazing ability to forget those who have shown respect toward us. How often is it that we recognize what we do for others and forget what others have done for us? We need to help children recognize those who have respect for them, and to recognize the methods by which respect has been shown. It is good to reflect back over the past day, or week, or month to see the ways in which you have been honored or admired, or recognized as a unique person. What compliments have you received, what preferences have you been shown? What honors have been bestowed upon you?

Well, then, these are the three dimensions: toward yourself, toward others, and from others. It is important that in each of the eight value categories we teach children and we teach ourselves to observe the processes of valuing that are occurring (or not occurring) day by day. The example that I have given has been in the category of respect. But I hope that you can see that the same three dimensions must be applied to the other seven value categories. In a real sense, we must learn to love ourselves, to love others, and to recognize the love we have received and are receiving from others. We must have self-control or power over ourselves. We must participate in the sharing and shaping of decisions made in groups, the sharing of power with others - recognize when others are allowing us to participate in the decision-making processes.

As a simple guide, I have outlined below a list of the objectives of the valuing process in terms of each of the dimensions described above.

I. Behavioral objectives related to the way a person improves his perception of himself:

- Liking yourself.
- Increasing self-esteem.
- Increasing one's own abilities (in social, thinking, communication, motor and aesthetic skills).
- Increasing knowledge of yourself and the world around you.
- Increasing participation in the decision-making process.
- Increasing both your goods and services to others.
- Increasing your physical and mental health.
- Increasing your sense of personal responsibility.

II. Behavioral objectives related to the way a person increases his perception of others.

- Liking and wanting to be a friend to others.
- Respecting another person.

- Helping others to discover and develop their talents.
- Helping others to increase their knowledge.
- Sharing opportunities for others to participate in making decisions.
- Helping others to find opportunities to increase their goods and services.
- Helping others to increase their own physical and mental health.
- Helping others to increase their sense of personal responsibility.

III. Behavioral objectives related to the way a person increases the perception he feels others have for him.

- Increasing your awareness of friendship that others have for you.
- Increasing your awareness of recognition, commendation or honors that others give to you.
- Increasing your awareness of skills you obtain from others.
- Increasing your awareness of knowledge you obtain from others.
- Increasing your awareness of the participation others may grant you in making decisions.
- Increasing your awareness of goods and services you receive from others.
- Increasing your awareness of physical and mental health you receive through others.
- Increasing your awareness of responsibility that others may wish to share with you.

IV. Behavioral objectives related to a balance of values.

- Avoiding long-term deprivations or over-indulgence.
- Helping others to avoid long-term deprivations or over-indulgence.
- Reducing the long-term deprivation or over-indulgence that others may develop toward you.

3

PRINCIPLES OF VALUING, Part 1

The process of valuing contains certain basic principles: *enhancement and deprivation, base and scope, a balanced life, a democratic goal,* and *shaping and sharing.* It will be important to describe briefly each one of these basic principles.

ENHANCEMENT AND DEPRIVATION

Values are not static entities, although each of us has the same needs; moreover, our status regarding the fulfillment of these needs is in a constant state of flux. At one point in time, we may be deprived in the area of skill. At the same moment we may be enhanced in the category of power, and even overly indulged in the category of affection. It therefore seems important not only to be able to identify the particular value area or value areas with which a person is concerned at the moment, but to understand the status of need fulfillment within each of these value categories.

Perhaps the following chart of a valuing continuum, developed by W. Ray Rucker, can help give some understanding to this concept, to this principle of *enhancement and deprivation.* The principle involved in the valuing process is that we are always moving ourselves and are assisting others to move in the direction of greater and greater enhancement or, in other words, toward full potential.

BASE AND SCOPE

The principle of *base and scope* in valuing can best be illustrated through a few practical examples. A young boy may take on a paper route in order to earn some money. His base value is wealth. However, his intentions are to use the money he is earning in order to buy himself a football. His base value is wealth (money) and the scope is also wealth (goods). Or let us say that he wanted the money to help finance his education. In this case, the base is wealth but the scope is enlightenment or skill. The base value is like a launch pad and the scope is the destination. For example, we may seek a position of leadership, not for power, but for respect. A young child will give away trinkets in order to buy friendship. A teacher will donate to a cause in order to gain influence or maintain respect. One child will teach a younger child a skill in order to gain respect. In each case, it is important to remember that often the values that we see on the surface are not the ultimate goals.

It is therefore important that we are able to distinguish between the base and the scope values. The question raised in value analysis, therefore, must not simply be what values do we see in another person as lacking and deprived, or indulged and overindulged, but why do we find them so? What values does a person

VALUE DEPRIVATION-ENHANCEMENT CONTINUUM

Developed by W. Ray Rucker

MOVEMENT TOWARD PATHOLOGY		LOW VALUE STATUS	MOVEMENT TOWARD FULL POTENTIAL		VALUE CATEGORY
Alienation Hatred	Fear Suspicion	Indifference Withdrawal	Caring Acceptance	Trust Intimacy	AFFECTION
Degradation Disintegration	Discrimination Segregation	Isolation Inferiority	Self-esteem Identity	Esteem of Others Integration	RESPECT
Incompetency Failure	Non-achievement Inadequacy	Under-achievement Awkwardness	Achievement Adequacy	Competency Success	SKILL
Distortion Deception	Confusion Misunderstanding	Uncertainty Ambiguity	Awareness Openness	Empathy Sharing	ENLIGHTENMENT
Resistance Aggression	Submission Coercion	Conformity Dependence	Self-direction Influence	Cooperation Participation	INFLUENCE (or Power)
Indigence Destitution	Non-productivity Marginal	Maintenance Subsistence	Productivity Creativity	Abundance Affluence	WEALTH
Anxiety Illness	Irritation Frustration	Existence Unhappiness	Hope Joy	Contentment Health	WELL-BEING
Malice Depravity	Irresponsibility Unscrupulousness	Apathy Negligence	Responsibility Consideration	Integrity Altruism	RESPONSIBILITY (or Rectitude)

seek, and what techniques and what values is the person using to achieve the values he seeks? It is more important to identify the scope value than the base value, for only in this way can we address ourselves to the underlying causes and basic needs rather than the surface symptoms. A kleptomaniac will take things that do not belong to him; however, to have the things he takes is not his need. A pyromaniac loves to watch fires; but neither is it his scope need to have a fire. Anger, hatred, enmity, strife, backbiting, and spite may all be base needs and are often dealt with as if they are underlying problems.

What is the scope purpose of hatred? Is it not respect? In fact, it seems that most if not all of the items previously mentioned relate to the deprivation of respect. There is a Biblical admonition that exemplified the principle I am attempting to describe. In the Old Testament it is said, "an eye for an eye and a tooth for a tooth".[3] In the New Testament Jesus says, "Love them that hate you, pray for them that despitefully use you."[4] When our concern is at the base level, we use hatred to fight hatred and strife to fight strife. The axiom I would propose is that deprivations breed deprivations and enhancements breed enhancements. If the root of hatred is a lack of respect, then by offering respect, building respect, strengthening respect, encouraging respect, we are placing the valuing process in action. The application to education is a simple one. Teachers must constantly remind themselves not to ask the question "What is Johnny doing?", but "Why is he doing it?" What are the areas of deprivation he seeks to fulfill? And what are the ways the teacher can use to help the child build and strengthen those areas of felt deprivation?

Again we must be reminded that this is a three-dimensional process. It requires that the teacher ask herself, "What can I do to help Johnny be enhanced?" Secondly, "What can Johnny do to help himself to be enhanced?" And thirdly, "How can Johnny recognize the ways in which others are enhanced or can help him become more enhanced?" In this way, we concentrate on the scope needs rather than the base needs of an individual child.

4

PRINCIPLES OF VALUING, Part 2

THE BALANCED LIFE

The third basic principle of the valuing process is the *balanced life*. As stated earlier, these eight value categories are interdependent; they are interwoven, intertwined; they are in many ways inseparable, although there are times in which they may be rank-ordered, or even be placed in a hierarchy of value needs.

There is another sense in which they must constantly be balanced. This balance is not an absolute balance. It is a relative balance. It is a dynamic balance. It is only over a long span of time (weeks, months, or years) that we should attempt to see a balance of the value categories. Alfred North Whitehead has indicated that he felt there was a kind of imbalance created during the early years of schooling. At the elementary level, the function of education was to be romance; that is, an excitement for learning, a delight in knowledge, a joy over the development of new ideas, the awareness of new ideas. He felt it was in the middle grades that emphasis should be placed on the development of skills; on precision, on the acquisition of the basic tools of learning — reading, writing, arithmetic, history, art and music — and that the upper grades should be concerned with what he called generalizations; that is, with learning to put all the pieces together, with synthesizing, at that stage in which inferences and applications and the formulation of new ideas can spring forth.[5]

Although I agree with the three major stages as described by Whitehead, it would be my contention that all three stages should be manifested in every class at every grade level, in every subject, every day of the classroom experience. I believe that every topic should begin with an element of romance and excitement. Once this romance has been established, skills and precision can then be formulated and acquired as needed; before any lesson has been completed, generalizations and applications to one's personal life and to the lives of others, and to society as a whole, should culminate the learning process. A life would be unbalanced if it concentrated on precision and neglected romance or generalization, or concentrated on romance and generalization and neglected precision, or concentrated on generalizations and precision and neglected romance.

In this same way, the valuing process requires a balancing of all eight basic value-needs. In terms of self-analysis, each child must learn to analyze his value status in all eight value areas. A child that is over-indulged in power and deprived in affection is unbalanced. A child who has the respect of others but is deprived of rectitude is unbalanced. A child who has great skill and enlightenment but is devoid of mental and physical well-being is unbalanced.

This same principle of the balanced life must also be applied to the classroom itself. There are classes where there is an extreme degree of affection shown for each of the members of the class, but little learning takes place. There are classes where the instructor and students are prepared to learn, where enlightenment and skill are available but air conditioning, lighting, chairs, desks, and supplies within the room make learning impossible. Thus there is an imbalance of potential enhancement in enlightenment and skill and a potential deprivation in mental and physical well-being. In the upper grades there is often a felt deprivation of influence among students. They want to make more decisions for themselves; they want to have some influence over the decisions that are made concerning what they study, where they study, how they study, when they study. The potential for enlightenment and skill development is high, but the deprivation of influence produces the unbalanced life within the classroom by making enlightenment and skill almost impossible.

There are, therefore, a few questions that a teacher again must raise in terms of the basic principles of the balanced life. The first is, "How does each one of my students see himself in terms of a balance of these eight value needs?" Individually, where are their felt deprivations, and how do the deprivations in certain value areas affect their ability to be enhanced in other areas? And, of course, the second question for the teacher to ask herself is, "Am I creating the possibility of a balanced life for the class as a whole?" In other words, do I show these students that I love them, that I care, that I am concerned? Do I show them that I respect them, do I

listen to them, am I willing to consider their ideas? Do I
share power? Do I allow them to manifest their own
skills and enlightenment? Is there a discussion of right
and wrong, and do I allow them to assume responsibilities for areas in which they can assume responsibility?

It has been said that teachers too often assume
responsibilities for their children in areas where children
can assume the responsibilities for themselves. In a
recent article concerning the patient/psychiatrist relationship, it was pointed out that the more responsibility
for the patient that the psychiatrist assumes, the less able
the patient is to stand on his own two feet,[6] and he
becomes more dependent upon the psychiatrist to solve
his problems. I feel that this principle also applies in the
classroom.

In a very real sense, a child at the point of birth is
almost wholly dependent upon the parent, the adult
authority, the external control. As the child progresses
toward maturity, toward adulthood, all value categories need to be continuously enhanced and the child
needs, in turn, to assume greater responsibility for
enhancement in all eight categories toward others. In
this fashion, the valuing process is conducive to a
balanced life — one that is continuously moving upward
toward greater and greater personal responsibility and
cooperative action. This leads to the next very important basic principle of the valuing process, the *democratic goal.*

THE DEMOCRATIC GOAL

No man is an island unto himself, particularly in a
democratic society. The democratic principle is that we
each have a responsibility for the whole. Democracy has

often been defined as a wide sharing of power. Each man has a vote and each vote is of equal importance. It is the voice of the majority that determines our corporate actions, policies, principles, and laws. The democratic goal of the valuing process is simply that the wide sharing of power is only one of eight, basic, important dimensions of the democratic process. Democracy is a wide sharing of affection and respect, of skill and enlightenment, of wealth and well-being, and of influence and responsibility.

Space permits but a few general examples of how each of these value categories are widely shared in a democratic society. Our many levels of government reflect our concern for a wide sharing of power and the scope of governmental agencies reflects our concern for well-being, enlightenment, and skill. The formation of our civic and service organizations provides an indication of our concern for a wide sharing of respect. The following quotation, taken from a plaque at the Statue of Liberty, is an indication of our concern for a wide sharing of affection:

Give me your tired, your poor,
Your huddled masses yearning to breathe free,
The wretched refuse of your teeming shore.
Send these, the homeless, tempest-tossed to me,
I lift my lamp beside the golden door!

Our concern that all those accused of crime receive a speedy trial by a jury of peers attests to our desire for a wide sharing of responsibility. Our processes are in no way perfect. But a democratic society does reflect a wide sharing of all human values and in this sense is a basic exemplar of the valuing process.

Now these same concepts of a democratic goal must be applied to the classroom level of education. How democratic is your classroom? It is possible and highly profitable for a class to evaluate itself as a democracy in miniature; to establish for itself its own rules of conduct, its own methods of recognizing respect and sharing affection; and even the wide sharing of influence within the classroom itself. I often ask teachers to assess the decisions that they allow children to make for themselves; and then to attempt as much as possible to allow children to assume a greater and greater role of the decision-making process within that classroom. In this way, the teacher becomes a learner among learners; a resource person rather than the teacher.

For a moment take a look at the physical arrangements within the classroom. Where is the teacher's desk? Is it at the head of the class or does she sit with the children? Are there independent learning centers, or does all learning center around the teacher's desk? Do children learn from the teacher or does the teacher and the class learn from one another? Does the teacher do all the teaching, or do the children assume much of the teaching responsibilities themselves? Can the teacher honestly say that she is learning as much from the children as they are learning from her? When rules are broken, who determines the penalties? Are they pre-set penalties, or are they determined on the spot? Are they subjectively or objectively determined? Are the goals for each class session, or ten-week period, or semester determined by the teacher, by the class, or together? Can the schedule be changed? Can children set their own independent goals for the work they accomplish or intend to accomplish? Can they set their own time limits for learning?

How flexible is the scheduling? Answers to questions like these reflect the degree of classroom democracy.

SHAPING AND SHARING

Another basic principle is the *shaping and sharing* of values.

Though a value area or need may have been satisfied once, it never remains satisfied. Skill is maintained through practice. Enlightenment is never fully attained; there is always more to know, more to understand. Each time a question is answered, more questions come to mind. Respect, like all of the other values, is a tenuous, delicate thing which seems to continuously ebb and flow and can easily be mangled, deformed and distorted out of proportion to what was originally intended.

It is, therefore, important to remind ourselves that values are continuously shaped and reshaped, adapted, corrected, and adjusted. It has been said that there is a thin line between love and hate. What was once a vital, pure, and holy love could, within a moment's notice, become hatred, anger and a destructive force. Power in its negative sense has been said to corrupt. However, power in a constructive, positive, enhancing way can be beneficial, but must constantly be guarded. Our democratic processes of checks and balances is a way to keep us from distorting and misusing, for selfish purposes, the values we hold. It is in this sense that the valuing process is an endless process.

Teachers at every grade level must remember that values need to be shaped and modeled every day of the school year. Historically, the teacher has been charged with the task of shaping the skills and the enlightenment of the child through her attitude, behavior, and classroom structure. She also, by omission or commission, continually molds and shapes the children's affection, respect, power, well-being, rectitude, and wealth, as well. Once again, however, it is important to recognize that the burden should not be upon the teacher but upon the child. Once the child recognizes the status of his own value needs and the areas of deprivation, he or she can begin to assume a greater responsibility in strengthening areas in which he is currently either deprived or feels a deprivation.

How does a child go about gaining affection from others? Are the methods used the best ones available? — the most enhancing toward himself and others? What new processes can be devised to mold a strong, positive, enhancing bond of affection? Is the child deprived in the area of self-control? What is the child doing now to establish a stronger degree of self-control? What are alternative methods that he can use to strengthen his self-discipline, hold back his anger, redirect his frustration, and utilize his energy for constructive purposes? These techniques are all part of learning to shape a person's value needs.

It would be one-sided, however, to concentrate on the shaping of values without also recognizing that the valuing process includes the sharing of values. Each one of us is linked together in many ways. There is hardly an act that you or I can perform which does not, in some way, impinge upon the lives of others. The very processes I use to shape, mold, strengthen, and enhance my own value needs will have an impact upon others. But valuing is more than this. It is also the deliberate attempt to share with others the value enhancements that you have gained and are continuing to gain for yourself. As I learn to love myself, I can learn to share that love with others. As I learn to develop greater self-respect, I can share respect with others. As I learn self-control, I can help others learn to control themselves.

Sharing takes on many forms. I think that one of its major avenues, however, is that of example, or *modeling*.[2] A poem I learned some years ago goes something like this:

I'd rather see a sermon than hear one any day;
I'd rather one should walk with me than merely tell the way.
The eye's a better pupil and more willing than the ear,
Fine counsel is confusing, but example's always clear;
And the best of all the preachers are the men who live their creeds,
For to see good put in action is what everybody needs.[7]

Parents more than anyone recognize how their words and actions are manifested in their own children, often to their own despair. We share what we are. People learn more by observing what we do than what we say.

Now, within the classroom there are at least two specific applications of the principles of sharing. The first, of course, is the modeling done by the teacher; and secondly, the modeling done by the children one to another. How often does a teacher stop to gain an honest feedback from her own class on how they see her? An interesting and informative experiment along this line is to ask the children to list independently the ten major roles that they see the teacher perform; or, as I have done with administrative groups, to ask teachers to have their children list the roles they see the principal perform. A simple value analysis of their responses can provide valuable insight as to whether the principal or teacher is seen as a model of a balanced life. All too often, however, a tabulation of these responses will indicate that the major concerns of a given teacher or principal are in the areas of responsibility, influence, and skill. Too few are seen as affectionate, respectful,

45

and happy. Where these areas of deprivation are identified within the classroom or within the school, strategies can then be established to strengthen the areas of identified deprivations.

Another area of shared values, from the standpoint of school administration and/or teacher-directed leadership, is in the development and application of the goals and objectives of the institution. Do the stated objectives oi the institution reflect a balanced concern for all eight value categories? Here again I think one will find that there is a heavy emphasis placed on enlightenment, skill and well-being, with an assumption that, in some magical fashion, the value goals of wealth, influence and respect will somehow be bestowed at a future unknown date. In what ways and in how many ways are children allowed to participate in the decision-making processes of the educational institution? In what ways are children given recognition, respect, admiration, and honor for achievements other than academic achievements and athletic achievements?

In one classroom, I remember, a teacher listed a "child of the week" on a front bulletin board where a picture and biographical information were presented. That child was then treated with special respect by the teacher and by the other members of the class throughout the week and he assumed much of the leadership in decisions that were made concerning the classroom. Every child within the room was given this opportunity for one week out of the school year.

I also know of a reception area in a certain principal's office where a different child is recognized each day of the school year (by a photograph and history of his qualities) as a unique individual with talents, skills, and hobbies; the child is thereby given special notification that he or she is unique. That day becomes his day within the school.

Before we leave this point of shaping and sharing values, I should also mention that I have found it profitable to encourage teachers to send students to the principal's office for outstanding achievements in academics, exemplary attitudes and behavior, and for things accomplished in the classroom. The principal is thus recognized as someone concerned and interested in the positive and enhancing aspects of children, as well as his normally-perceived role as a disciplinarian. This practice, of course, requires a prior understanding of its purpose by the principal and a concerted effort by all members of the teaching staff to utilize the technique as often as possible.

Another extension of this practice is the technique of sending notes home to parents in recognition of a child's performance. A teacher or principal often recognizes the sharing of affection, respect, power, etc. among students and can note such incidences and draft a simple note to be sent home to the parent in recognition of the performance observed. In this fashion, the parent also gains an impression of the teacher, or principal as not just a disciplinarian, but as a loving, enhancing, encouraging individual who recognizes and rewards constructive behavior — the kind that makes our society a democratic process in practice as well as in theory.

The second aspect of sharing as a basic principle is the sharing that can occur and does occur among the students themselves. It seems to me that *value sharing by students* should not be a haphazard activity. It should be a concerted effort, made on a very systematic basis; and to this end I would suggest that, first of all, a teacher concentrate on developing within her students an understanding of only one of the value categories at a time. Tunnel vision in this sense is very important. A focus on one value area; in fact, even on one dimension of one value area, is by far the most productive approach.

We can use as an example the second dimension, that of sharing values toward others, and concentrate on the one value area of affection. It might be possible for a teacher to ask the children to observe during one day the sharing of affection, of one child toward another, as they observe it on the playground or on the way to school, or even within their own home. In this way, they become more aware of the category of affection (caring, concern, friendship, fondness) as it is shared from one individual toward another, and can easily describe those areas and situations where the sharing takes place. Note that I do not recommend the sharing of times in which values are withheld or deprived. It is important, also, to recognize that a deliberate effort to be enhancing in a focused way, that is in one value category, will have a beneficial spinoff effect in all other value categories. The so-called Hawthorne effect will be seen almost immediately. An individual enhanced in skill will also exhibit enhancement in affection, respect, and well-being.

5

STEPS IN VALUING

I would suggest that it is important to begin with the development of a conceptual knowledge and proceed as quickly as possible to an experiential knowledge. Although all of the steps between concept and experience cannot be easily spelled out, the following factors appear to be important:

(a) There should be a basic understanding of the synonyms that can be used for a particular value category and every child should learn to develop the ability to communicate a beginning definition for that value area.

(b) Children should learn the ability to identify the enhancement, sharing, withholding, and deprivation of a particular category in distinct situations outside of themselves.

(c) Children should develop the ability to identify any enhancement and sharing within that same category in more personally-related situations and be able to share these with others in the classroom setting.

(d) Once there has been established a basic understanding of synonyms and an identification of value enhancement and deprivations outside of themselves and in personally-related situations, it is important that the children learn to identify enhancement, sharing, withholding, and deprivations of that particular value category within themselves. A child may then be able to understand the meaning of the word skill, to see skills exercised by people in the community, to identify skills that they themselves are developing — those in which they are strong, and those they need yet to develop. Note that, if you stop here, the process has only provided enlightenment; you must ask the students to select deprived areas within themselves and to commit themselves to finding ways in which to become more enhanced.

(e) It is then important that students develop a knowledge of the ways by which a person can become deprived of a particular value category along with an analysis of the ways by which an individual can deprive himself and others in that given value category.

How does a person deprive himself of affection? What are the attitudes and behavior that cause one person not to like another? How does one who is disliked bring this situation upon himself and others? What does a person do that causes you not to like him? Can you identify the attitudes and behavior that cause the resulting deprivation of affection?

(f) Finally, and most importantly, the children should develop a knowledge of the ways by which a person is enhanced in a particular value category, along with an understanding or analysis of the ways by which an individual can be enhancing toward others and toward himself. The valuing process is one of recognition, of value enhancements and deprivations, of growth, of always moving toward enhancement and personal experience, i.e. of putting oneself in very practical ways into the process of value-sharing and value-shaping. The valuing process should not be treated as an indoctrination, but rather as one of value understanding and development. Impartation of your own beliefs and standards must be accompanied by an openness to examine those of others and a willingness for self-correction wherever non-enhancing value positions are revealed within yourself.

There are certain procedures that we ask teachers to develop within their classrooms in order to make the principles of valuing available to the student. I would like, briefly, to cover in simplified fashion an understanding of each of these processes.

6

PROCESSES IN VALUING, Part 1

GOAL-SETTING

Goal-setting is an important part of valuing. As stated earlier, goal-setting must begin with two categories of goals: goals that are set by the teacher (assigned goals), and goals that are set by the student (independent goals). It is assumed that, as the children become more attuned to the concept of goal-setting, the quantity of assigned goals will lessen and the quantity of independent goals will increase.

The procedure, simply stated, is that each child will have in front of him a daily goal-sheet for the week. The subject-matter areas are listed across the top of the page and the days of the week listed down along the left-hand column. On a certain day of the week (usually Friday or Monday), a set of assigned goals is established for each day of the week and put on the board to be copied onto the daily goal sheets by the students. The assigned goals should be stated as specifically as possible, listing pages to be read or assignments to be completed, or questions to be answered. The independent goals, on the other hand, should be devised by the students, with some initial guidance, perhaps, from the teacher. Under language arts, for example, students may say that on Tuesday they will read a story about Lincoln. Under the category of reading, they may say that on Wednesday they will read 10 pages from a certain book. Under the topic of mathematics, they might list something like copying six math problems from a certain page in the book, making up ten math questions of their own, and answering all of them. Under physical education they may list something like "play Capture the Flag." At the end of each week, each child should evaluate his own progress toward achieving his assigned and independent goals. The following six questions can be posed (and it is preferred that they be given to the children weekly so they can have in mind the questions that they will use to evaluate themselves):

1. Did you complete the goals set for each day? List your answer in terms of a percentage.

2. Were your goals set too high, so that you could not reach them? If so, what specific suggestions can you make for confining your stated goals to those you can complete?

3. Were your goals set so low that they were not challenging enough? If so, what specific suggestions can you make that would help establish more challenging ones?

4. Were your goals specific enough, so that you could reach them easily? If not, what things can you suggest to make your goals more specific?

5. Did you set a time limit for reaching your goals? What specific suggestions can you make that would

allow you to set time limits for next week?

6. What have you learned this week that will help you in setting goals for next week?[8]

Answers to this latter question will probably consist of a recap of suggestions made in response to the previous five questions.

Goal-setting is an extremely important component of valuing. Because it places the burden and responsibility of learning upon the child rather than upon the teacher, the teacher becomes more of a resource person than a supervisor of learning — a guide rather than a control.

PROBLEM SOLVING

Problem-solving is the second important process in the valuing approach. It is my opinion that very practical problems applicable to children should be created or devised by the children themselves and that these problems should be explored by the class in order to learn the processes of problem solving. For example, what does a child do when he loses his lunch money? What does a child do when he is called "chicken" or placed in a position where he is expected to fight back? What does a child do when he doesn't understand an assignment that has been given to him? All of these problems, and many others, are faced by children every day, and they, are unaware for the most part, how to go about solving them.

The techniques of problem solving are a crucial responsibility of the educational process and an integral part of valuing in the classroom. There are many different approaches that can be used for learning the skills of problem solving.

One simple process of problem solving, described by Arnspiger, Rucker, and Preas, outlines five component operations described as (1) the clarification of the goal, (2) the description of the past trends, (3) the analysis of existing conditions, (4) the projection of future developments if the condition is not rectified, (5) the invention of alternatives and their scientific appraisal in terms of value — enhanced or deprived.[9] I might add two additional steps as follows: (6) the selection of an alternative for trial purposes, and (7) the evaluation of that alternative, which might call for recycling back to step (5) and the selection of another alternative for experimentation.

In any type of problem, it is important first of all to identify the goal that you are attempting to reach. What is it that you want as an ultimate objective? Can you spell it out in some simplified terms? To do so could conceivably include the determination of some intermediate goals, or steps on the way toward the ultimate objective. Once you know the goal, trend-thinking will help clarify the depth of the problem. This involves the identification of past events that have led up to the problem that now exists.

A question to ask in this connection is, "Has this problem existed for a long period of time, or is it a fairly recent one?" The purpose of this question is to gain some insight into the extent to which it is a major problem, one that must be tackled immediately. Condition-thinking is an analysis of the kinds of conditions that co-exist with the problem itself. Who is involved? How much is involved? How can we describe the problem in its present condition succinctly and yet comprehensively? Does everyone involved agree upon the status of the problem as it exists?

It is interesting to note that often in labor-management negotiations, one of the primary steps is to have management draft a statement of the problem as they see it and, at the same time, have labor draft a statement of the problem as they see it. These papers are then exchanged for rephrasing and returned for review and recycling, so that at some point management and labor can come to terms as to an agreed statement of the real problem.

The same steps can be utilized in goal thinking. Can management draft the goals of labor as they see them? Can labor in turn draft the goals of management as they see them? These goal statements can then be given to the opposite teams for clarification. Does management actually see their goals in terms of the way that labor has stated them (and vice versa)? This process may be repeated several times until there is a clear understanding of the goals as perceived by each side. Might not this same process be applicable in the classroom between competing or conflicting groups or individuals?

Once we have a clear understanding of the past trends and existing conditions, it is then possible to do some projective thinking; that is, to ask ourselves what, if the existing conditions continue without any interference or intervention, are the possibilities of their worsening or rectifying themselves, independent of any real intervention?

It is at this point that we are able to determine whether alternatives are needed and what these possible alternatives might be. It is necessary that the list of possible alternatives be left as wide-ranging as possible. I like to have children *list alternatives* without debate so that we can list on a chalkboard or on chart paper all of the possible alternatives that can be devised without discussion. It is then possible to go back and combine certain kinds of alternatives that appear to be similar in nature, to eliminate those alternatives which seem completely unfeasible, and to list in rank order the alternatives that seem best for further consideration.

Although the processes of problem solving and the skills of problem solving take a considerable amount of time when used in this fashion, they lay a foundation for very efficient problem solving skills once so learned. In fact, if you reflect on the problems you have solved, you will find you often do them in your mind without serious deliberation, and that many problem-solving activities are performed by you in a matter of seconds rather than in hours or days.

The point here is simple: children for the most part do not know how to solve problems. They tend toward tunnel-vision, seeing only one solution to a given problem. This is so prevalent in our society today, that in my personal opinion, problems such as juvenile delinquency, drug abuse, divorce, family disintegration, deception, fraud, shoplifting, and many other such high-risk/low-gain manifestations of behavior are directly traceable to an incapacity for solving problems. It is urgent, therefore, that the skills of problem solving be established early, and in the classroom, and that they be established in ways that are the most enhancing to the individual and to the group.

I have said very little, up to this point, about the concept of *problem solving* as it relates to the valuing process; and I must, in some fashion, relate these two. Once an alternative has been chosen using the skills of problem solving, it is important to evaluate an alternative selected on the basis of the valuing process. Questions such as the following may be appropriate: Does the alternative selected allow for the greatest enhancement of affection, respect, skill, etc., for the individual, the other party or parties involved, and for society as a whole? Since our objective is enhancement, it is important that our selection of an alternative be one that produces the greatest amount of enhancement.

MODELING

A third process of valuing which we have discussed in some depth earlier is *the process of modeling*. Volumes have been written on the importance of the example or the modeling concept as an integral part of the development of the individual. It is possible to take each one of the value categories and reflect as a teacher upon ways you could model it before your class. Many teachers in our workshops have done just that; and I would like to suggest some ways in which you can be a model of the valuing process within the classroom.

Under the category of affection, for instance, a smile of welcome at the beginning of the day, compliments to children as they are merited, and written personal comments on work would be effective examples of modeling. I have encouraged teachers to write a personal note to two or three different children each day and to place these notes on the children's desks, folded over and taped down, so that everyone in the class knows that there are two or three children who have received a personal comment. The children themselves can keep these notes confidential if they so desire. These personal comments should be the most enhancing and most honest responses that you can give to children. They might be comments upon the work they have done, or the attitude that they have shown, or upon their

59

enthusiasm, or upon the progress they have made. Each of us needs to daily experience some degree of recognition and success. Children, especially, need to sense and receive from their own teachers such personal recognition as often as possible, and the modeling that you provide by giving personal comments very soon creates spinoff effects. This we have observed in many classrooms where, for example, the children have asked permission (of the teacher or the class) to pass enhancing written comments to other children.

As a demonstration of modeling in the category of responsibility, teachers setting up classroom jobs should have those jobs assigned on a rotating basis, so that everyone has a chance to be a classroom helper. In fact, it is possible in many classes to allow children to make those assignments for themselves. It is also possible to give the class a choice of three activities that need to be finished in a given period of time. These assignments can be done in the order they independently choose. This builds a degree of responsibility.

For a total-class project you may wish to set up a bank in which you use, not real money, but play money, allowing everyone to be given initially the same amount of money. The children can then buy services from one another from this bank. As an individual project, you might select a special day for the display of personal wealth, wealth meaning both goods and services. Make sure, however, that every individual is allowed to display some degree of wealth on his particular day. Special music is also a sharing of wealth. You can teach the children a favorite song or you can allow them to teach one another songs.

THE "I" MESSAGE

In modeling, it is necessary that you practice being positive and enhancing. In this connection, I have devised a list of deprivational statements which I have asked teachers to rewrite into enhancing statements. Here is one example of a deprivational statement: "If you won't do what the class is doing then you are too little to be in this class." I have asked teachers to use the following three principles in rewriting such statements:

(1) *Use an "I" message rather than a "you" message.* By that I mean you should begin your statement by indicating your feelings about the situation. Say something like this, for instance: "I feel that you are not doing the assignment that has been given to the entire class and this makes me unhappy or sad."

(2) *Try and deal with the issue and not with the character of the individual.* There is no way for the child to protect himself when you say, "You are too little to be in this class." His only response is to retreat, admitting that he is too little, or to fight back by saying he is not too little. There is nothing specific in the statement that he can deal with. Therefore, don't use character assassination — deal with the issue. The issue is not that he is too little. The issue may be that he does not know what to do or how to do it, and he needs help rather than criticism. What is it that the class is doing? Does he understand the assignment? Does he know how to complete the assignment? Does he need help from another student or the teacher?

(3) *Offer constructive direction or assistance.* To begin by saying, "If you won't do what the class is doing —" is to imply that the child knows what to do and how to do it. It would be better to offer some direction for the child

61

so that he can complete the assignment, or to allow him to be teamed up with someone else that knows how to do the assignment.

Modeling involves using communication that is positive and enhancing rather than deprivational and destructive, and the "I" message is an important tool of such communication. One of the most complete treatises on "I" messages is to be found in the book *Between Parent and Child*.[10]

Many of us in education have been told to use the word "I" sparingly because it sounds rather self-centered if it is overused. Consequently, it is hard for many teachers to become accustomed to the idea that there are occasions, many occasions, when it is better to say "I" than to say "you." One such occasion is when a class arouses the teacher's anger. An "I" message, or the lack of it, can affect each of the eight basic value needs. If a teacher, for instance, is angered and says, "You are always making mistakes and causing trouble," he gives students a sense of deprivation in one or more of the value categories. The word "you" can be taken to mean a general group or a single student. Frequently when the group as a whole is referred to as "you" students interpret it to mean the singular and they take it personally. "I" messages usually do not single out a person but they can carry much impact because they describe a teacher's feelings more strongly.

Positive "I" messages can be enhancing in the value categories. If a teacher says, for instance, "I am proud of your work and I think I have a fine class," the class will then tend to share enhancement and affection, respect, well-being, and possibly all of the other value categories. A negative "I" message, on the other hand, can deprive children in their needs.

Many of the messages that we send to people about their behavior are "you" messages, messages that are directed at the other person and have a high probability of putting them down, of making them guilty, of making them feel their needs are not important, and generally making them tend to resist change. Examples of "you" messages are usually orders or commands. "Stop doing that." "Get into the car." Or name-calling statements such as, "You are acting like a baby," or "You are driving me crazy." Or statements that tend to give solutions: "You should forget that idea." "You'd better reconsider that idea," thereby removing the responsibility of decision-making for behavioral change away from the other person.

Perhaps the worst kind of "you" message is the "if" message — the threat. "If you don't, then I will —." An "I" message, on the other hand, allows a person who is affected by the behavior of another to express the impact that it has on him and at the same time to leave the decision and responsibility for modifying the behavior with the person who demonstrated that particular behavior.

An "I" message consists of three parts: (1) the specific message, (2) the resulting feeling others experience because of that message, and (3) the tangible effects on you. Thus a teacher might say to a student, in terms of the message, "When you rap on your desk with your pencil I feel upset (feeling level) because I get distracted and have difficulty teaching" (effect level). Or, a wife might say to her husband, "When I try to help you and you don't say anything, I feel confused (feeling level) because I don't know how you feel about my help" (effect level). In essence the message allows the sender to say implicitly, "I trust you to decide what change in behavior is necessary."

In this manner, "I" messages build relationships and, equally important, they do not place the sender in the position of enforcing the new behavior, as is frequently the case with the "you" message mentioned above. "I" messages therefore are enhancing. "You" messages are generally deprivational. The valuing process implies that teachers and students alike are moving toward using enhancing statements — "I" messages — rather than deprivational statements — "you" messages.
"you" messages.

It is a valuable exercise to listen to television or the radio or read from articles in books and magazines, or to listen to one another and to be able to separate those messages which are "you" messages from those which are "I" messages. Decipher for yourself which tend to be enhancing and which tend to be deprivational. When deprivational statements are identified, practice rewording them into enhancing "I" messages.

7

PROCESSES IN VALUING, Part 2

ACTIVE LISTENING

The valuing process includes another very important concept. That is the concept of being aware of where children are and how they see things. It involves a degree of *active listening*. A book on listening written a decade ago by Nichols, is a book I would recommend to all teachers.[11] He indicates that active listening involves sitting on the edge of your chair, symbolically, and a rise in your body temperature; not just paying attention, but having your mind alert.

Your mind is able to receive information at least three times faster than your ears are able to pick up the spoken word. Normally, a man speaks at the rate of about 120 words per minute. The mind, however, is able to comprehend at the rate of over 400 words per minute. Active listening, therefore, involves being able to mull over the words that are spoken "between the words as they are spoken." This is using your mind to the fullest. It is actively listening to children.

The valuing process implies that the person I am relating to is worthy of my attention. He or she is important. I tell teachers that it is more important to give children quality time than quantity time. By that I mean, two minutes of your undivided attention is more important than five hours of passive listening.

OPEN COMMUNICATION

Open communication goes hand in hand with active listening. In this connection, a set of exercises dealing with encouraging communication and inhibiting communication in terms of each of the eight value categories has been established. The process is a very simple one and can be applied to each of the eight value categories.

I usually recommend that teachers begin with the deprivational side, the roadblocks to each of the categories, by listing all the words or phrases that would indicate behavioral and/or attitudinal evidences of blocked or inhibited communication. For example, sarcasm, insincerity, moralizing, insensitivity, no eye contact, ridicule, curt answers, untruthfulness, and closed-mindedness are some of the words and phrases that are roadblocks to the category of respect.

Once children have established as many words or phrases that indicate roadblocks to the category of respect, the next step would be to have them read over each of the roadblocks that they have filled in, placing a check mark next to those they themselves perceive to be part of their own attitude or behavior, and then to select one of the checked roadblocks that they will attempt to change or alleviate in and out of the classroom during the next week. If you can enlist your students in the recognition and elimination of roadblocks to communication you will have gone a long way toward establishing the valuing process in the lives of your students.

Although I often begin with the deprivational side of the thought processes concerning these value categories, I encourage the technique to *always end on the enhancement side*. The process remains essentially the same. The children are asked to fill in words or phrases that represent behavioral or attitudinal evidences of open or free communication or enhancement in a particular category. Again, let us say the category is respect; the words or phrases will be, for the most part, the opposite of those that they have identified as roadblocks; e.g., eye contact, truthfulness, sincerity, empathetic listening, honest praise, open-mindedness, and being positive. Once again, after establishing their list of positive or enhancing statements, they should be asked to read over that list, to check those items they perceive to be part of their own attitude and behavior, and to select one additional step that they will work on or develop in and outside the classroom the following week. As you can see, the implications of this technique for each of the eight value categories are of enormous importance.

What are the phrases and words we use that block affection and friendship between individuals? What are those things that cause us to build a caring relationship? What are the things that deprive others of a sense of well-being and enhance others with a sense of well-being? What are the deviations and enhancements in the category of power, or rectitude, or skill, or enlightenment? To spend one week on each of these eight value categories, identifying the things that block and those that enhance, will allow children to experience both an awareness of the negative aspects and an awareness of the positive aspects of the valuing process. In these ways we build open communication within the classroom.

DECISION MAKING

Decision making is another important process of valuing. Human beings have the unique ability to delay a decision. We can discuss problems, we can criticize the current situation, we can pose alternative solutions. But when it comes down to performing some action in making a decision, we often falter. Therefore one of the important processes of valuing is to help children learn how to make decisions, not just solve problems — to reach a decision after a review of all possible alternatives and to carry out the decision reached. Here, it may be important to refer back to the three-dimensional concept described earlier. In which of the value areas can we make decisions concerning movement toward greater enhancement?

At any time it could become important to identify an area of deprivation within ourselves; of enlightenment for instance, and then to make a decision concerning enhancing ourself in that particular area and committing ourself to it. It is good to write down the facts of the matter. If at this moment I considered myself to be deprived in the area of enlightenment, I could commit myself to gain enlightenment in a particular way over a set period of time using these particular strategies or techniques; and at a time specifically stated, I would evaluate my progress toward enhancing myself in the area of enlightenment. Or maybe we can identify an area of value deprivation in another person and proceed immediately, using the same strategies and techniques, to be more enhancing toward that person.

During the summer months, while teaching at the University of California, I have had each student concentrate on a particular member of his own family that he expects to spend some time with during the following weekend, then write down the value deprivation that he perceives in the other person, and describe a course of action he will take to become more enhancing. Before he returns to school on Monday, he makes an evaluation of his effectiveness in bringing a greater enhancement to that person. In class we then discuss, without mentioning names, the methods we used and the failures and successes achieved during the previous weekend.

It is important that each of us recognize that we are moving forward, that we are accomplishing goals, that we are fulfilling the needs of ourselves and others. It is sad that most of us spend a great deal of time muddling through life, never stopping to reflect upon our own accomplishments or the ways in which we have helped others. The processes of decision-making relative to valuing help us to see the ways in which we are beneficial to ourselves and others, and thereby to gain for ourselves a greater sense of self-respect and usefulness.

8

PROCESSES IN VALUING, Part 3

MEMORY APPRAISAL

There are many other processes that we use in valuing. There is neither space, nor time, nor the necessity to review them all here; but I would, however, like to describe another method that can be employed on an individual basis in order to gain a better perception of the long-range balance or imbalance in the value categories. This process is called *memory appraisal.*[12] The technique of memory appraisal was developed by Dr. Arnspiger over an eleven-year research study conducted at East Texas State University in a program of general studies.

The process consists of three separate phases. Phase I is, first of all, the recalling of events from the past. You are asked to record, beginning with your earliest remembrance, events of your lifetime. Be brief in recording these events. Record all of the content of your consciousness until you have covered fifty events. Once you have recalled fifty events from your past, prepare them in some ordered fashion. The first step will be to number each event chronologically. These numbers will provide reference points for the events in the later value coding and appraisal. Alongside each event, it is essential that your approximate age at the time of the event be recorded.

The next step is to go back over each event in order and value-analyze its consequences to yourself. It is helpful at this point to make a record chart having four columns across the top of the page headed as follows: column 1, the eight value categories, column 2, deprivation-event numbers, column 3, indulgence (or enhancement) event numbers, and column 4, over-indulgence event numbers. Then as you look at each event that you have recorded, 1 through 50, write down in the appropriate column under each value category the number representative of the event, judging each as either an enhancement, a deprivation, or an over-indulgence to you as you perceived it at the time that it took place. Once you have value-analyzed the consequences of each for yourself, you should then review all fifty events again, this time from the standpoint of their consequences for any and all other persons involved in the situation. Ask yourself how the occurrences were perceived from the viewpoint of these people. (Use a second copy of the record chart format.)

The third step is to compare the memory-appraisal record you have made from your own vantage point with the memory-appraisal of events made from the vantage point of the others involved, and to evaluate in a third record, the consequences for yourself in light of the new knowledge you now have of the way other persons viewed the situation at the time.

Possibly, a simple illustration of this technique will suffice.

A child, at the age of nine, was promised a piano on his tenth birthday. Just before his birthday arrived, his mother died and the money that had been saved for the piano was used for his mother's funeral. The child felt a deprivation in power because he could not control what took place, a deprivation in respect because his father did not fulfill his promise, a deprivation in wealth because he did not gain the piano promised him, a deprivation in skill because he did not have the piano to practice on, a deprivation in well-being because of his hurt feelings, a deprivation of rectitude because of the lack of responsibility on the part of the father (as the child perceived it), and a deprivation of affection in not receiving what he had been promised. There were, from the standpoint of the child, no enhancements in this particular situation and certainly no overindulgences. However, when this same situation is reviewed in the light of the consequences for the father and the mother, the placement of that particular event shifts into other categories. For example: from the standpoint of the father, there was a deprivation in power because he also could do nothing about the situation. There was a deprivation in his respect because he could not fulfill his promise. There was a deprivation of wealth because he had to choose between the piano and the funeral and he could not provide both. There was certainly a deprivation in well-being from the loss of his wife and the hurt he gave his son through not being able to fulfill his promise, and a deprivation in rectitude because of his inability to do the "right" thing for everyone involved.

There certainly was not any enhancement or any over-indulgence in that particular situation from the stand-point of the father. He was deprived as badly as, or worse than, his son.

Having made the above analysis, it would be obvious, first of all, that none of the deprivations imposed upon you (assuming you were the boy in our example) were deliberate on the part of your father, although at the age of nine you may have felt that way. You perceived them to be the result of deliberate attempts on his part to deprive you, rather than consequences over which he had little or no control. It is conceivable that, as this child, you could have harbored ill feelings against your father and mother for many years, and undeservedly so. The process of memory appraisal would allow you to reassess from a more mature vantage point the situation as it actually occurred, and thereby to assume a more enhancing position in light of your new ability to weigh past events.

Although I do not recommend that the processes of memory appraisal be used with children, I do feel that it is profitable for teachers to use the process of memory appraisal to view their own attitudes toward events in their lives. As a person thinks in his heart, so is he. The events of our past fashion, in many subconscious ways, our present performance. A teacher is a product of all the past experiences that she has had. It is, therefore, important that you assess and reassess the way you perceive yourself and the way you perceive others, looking at yourself so that you will be better able to recognize the ways in which you may have misinterpreted the events of your life from a lack of maturity. Teachers who have gone through this experience have seen for themselves that many of the ways they treat children are an outgrowth of ways they themselves had been treated, that their behavior had, in fact, been a rebellion against the way they had been treated.

As stated earlier, I believe that deprivations breed deprivations and enhancements breed enhancements. If you, as a teacher, have experienced deprivations, those deprivations tend to be repeated by you in your associations with other adults and with children. If, however, your past has been one of enhancement and you feel a high degree of it, then your reactions towards adults and to children alike will be those of enhancement. It is, therefore, vital that you are able to identify areas of your own life where you have felt deprivations and be able to analyze whether those felt deprivations were real or unreal, whether they were justified or unjustified, whether they were perceived from a lack of maturity, or whether they were valid and should have been dealt with in some positive fashion.

The utilization of memory appraisal has been an effective first step in the building within an individual of a more positive, enhancing outlook upon life — and in the production of a more positive, enhancing teacher in the classroom.

THE ANECDOTAL RECORD

It is difficult for me to leave the topic of the valuing process without covering one more useful approach, i.e., the *anecdotal record*. As we use it in our current workshops,[13] this is an assignment that begins immediately and is due the ninth meeting of the workshop. We encourage teachers to bring their anecdotal record with them for possible discussion during each of the workshop sessions. The process is simply to select a student to follow for at least two or three times a week during the nine-week period, and to work to enhance that student in those areas where deprivation is identified by the teacher. We ask the teachers to use a fictitious name for every person mentioned in the record and to avoid the identification of actual locations or times whenever possible.

The record contains three major sections: (1) a description of the anecdotal child. This section, to be written between the first and second workshop sessions, is to contain a brief overview of the physical features of the child: age, size, weight, height, hearing, health, etc.; (2) problems of coordination, language, attention span, home behavior, etc.; (3) classroom behavioral diffi- culties such as inability to adhere to rules, aggressive- ness, shyness, lying, cheating, rudeness, and poor academic performance or personal habits; (4) the teacher's evaluation, in terms of value categories, of the underlying areas of deprivation behind the student's surface behavior and attitudes seen; and (5) the teacher's selection of one value area within which she will attempt to assist that child to become more enhanced.

The second section of the record carries the actual anecdotal material. This section, to be written between the second and the eighth workshop sessions, is to contain the date, when appropriate, the time of the day that each incident took place, a description of the incident, and a value analysis *from the standpoint of the child;* that is, for example, a minus in affection if the class laughed at him, a plus in enlightenment if he learned his spelling words, a minus in power if he lost his self-control; and, lastly, a description of the strategies and techniques the teacher can or shall employ to enhance that child in the value area selected earlier.

The third and final section of the anecdotal record, to be written between the eighth and ninth workshop sessions, is to contain: (1) a summary chart of all the enhancements and deprivations recorded during the keeping of the anecdotal record; (2) a concluding statement evaluating progress made toward helping the child to be enhanced; (3) a concluding statement embodying the teacher's perception of the child's own awareness of his deprivations, his alternatives, his decision skills, and his sense of responsibility; and (4) any recommendations the teacher may have that could be implemented by the child himself, by the next teacher, a counselor, the parents, or by other significant persons in that child's life.

In order to make the anecdotal record concept more clear, I would like to give below some examples of each of the three sections of the anecdotal record.

Section A. Don is ten years old, about 4 feet, 10 inches tall, overweight, has short, dark brown hair, blue eyes, and is larger than most boys in the room. He is handsome, walks in a slow manner, is usually the last student out of the room, is usually well-dressed; shirt, pants, and socks are well-coordinated. He rarely smiles and is always complaining about students picking on him. He is bright and intelligent but appears somewhat confused, immature, and he even uses baby talk at times. He is not socially accepted by his peers, he argues constantly, and uses foul language. He seems to have a low opinion of himself. He keeps saying, "I'm dumb. I can't do the work."

I consider respect to be his major area of deprivation. I intend to assist him to develop his self-respect and his respect toward others, and to develop his recognition of the respect that he receives from others.

Section B. When everyone was present, Laura told the teacher that she had lost a plastic stick-on that was part of her toy set. A boy said he saw Don with it this morning. The usual morning hum before everyone settles down was abruptly silenced as a few faces turned toward Don. Don experienced a minus in respect because they all think he took it. He experienced a minus in affection: "They always say it's my fault, because they don't like me." He experienced a minus in well-being: "I am very sad because I have no friends."

I have to find ways to help Don to be accepted by the group. Perhaps Don could share his skill in adding with those other students that are having problems in math and thereby gain affection, friendship and respect.

Section C. My introduction represents a picture of Don prior to my enrollment in this course. Although positive changes occurred prior to the workshop, change became more rapid and more noticeable with the application of valuing. Don is really a changed person. He no longer lacks initiative; he volunteers readily and produces quality work. He smiles more often and increasingly assumes responsibility, not only in the class, but for his actions outside the class. He has dramatically improved his sense of responsibility and self-respect. This has had a positive effect on those students around him. His progress in other classes seems to be slower than in mine. However, it is a steady progress.

Perhaps the atmosphere of success in our room serves as a limited inspiration. He became aware of his deprivations in responsibility and respect through our studies of the eight value areas and has worked hard to find ways to enhance himself and others. Total class activities suggested in the workshop sessions and individual work with Don have really paid off.

I have shared the valuing approach with his parents and have placed a copy of this anecdotal record in his "cum" folder. I plan to share my feelings, findings, and ideas with his teacher for next year so she may continue to find the same success in meeting his needs that has so changed his attitude and behavior in the past ten weeks.

References for Section One

1. Proverbs 23:7
2. Lindlahr, Victor H., *You Are What You Eat*, Newcastle Publishing Company.
3. Exodus 21:24
4. Matthew 5:44
5. Whitehead, Alfred North, *The Aims of Education*, New York: The Macmillan Company, 1929.
6. Resnick, Robert W., "Chicken Soup is Poison", Reprint provided by Dr. H. O. Brayer, Orange County Department of Education, Drug Abuse Prevention Education Center, Santa Ana, California.
7. Guest, Edgar A., From the poem "Sermons We See".
8. Kalson, Stan, quoted in a tape presentation on the application of the Valuing process in a 5th Grade classroom, Palos Verdes Elementary School, Palos Verdes, California, Circa 1971.
9. Arnspiger, V. Clyde; Rucker, W. Ray; and Preas, Mary E., *Personality in Social Process*, Dubuque: Wm. C. Brown Book Company, 1969. (Now out of print.)
10. Ginott, Haim G., *Between Parent and Child*, New York: Avon Books, 1965.
11. Nichols, Ralph, and Stevens, Leonard, *Are You Listening?* McGraw-Hill Book Company, New York: 1954.
12. Rucker, W. Ray; Arnspiger, V. Clyde; and Brodbeck, Arthur J., *Human Values in Education*, Dubuque: Kendall/Hunt Publishing Company, 1969. (Available from Pennant Educational Materials.)
13. This record keeping assignment is required of all participants of the "Teaching for Responsible Behavior" workshops conducted by the Drug Abuse Prevention Education Center, Orange County Department of Education, Santa Ana, California.

SECTION TWO

MATERIALS AND STRATEGIES FOR TEACHERS

9

GAMES: A Valuable Educational Tool

The process of learning and gaming are identical in many ways. For most students especially the slow learners and the rebellious, the playing of educational games (with some supplemental activities) may be one of the best ways for learning. "The impulse to play games is part of a child's basic nature. Playing is what he does in his free time. It is one of the ways of investigating the world on his own."[7]

Games awaken a child's eagerness to learn, and require him to think, to imagine, to listen, to create, and to express his own ideas. Teachers have often discovered that a child's indifference or even his hostility to study is overcome by the playing of a game. And the game itself may be the best method that could be used to help the child learn the subject that he is attempting to cover within the classroom.

Perhaps we can best appreciate the value and importance of games if we think of the skills that we all need in our daily life, and the problems that arise through an inability to read, speak, write, or use our influence correctly. Horwitz and Goddard remind us of the importance of educational games when they make the following statement: "Have you ever wondered how it is that some people always seem to have just the words they need in any situation? And have you noted how often those individuals have the power to articulate their thoughts and desires clearly, to argue convincingly, to describe precisely, to tell a story interestingly, and tend to generally command respect and gain positions of prestige and influence?"[7] Think for a moment of the problems that arise from a lack of clarity in language which games can develop.

There are many benefits derived from playing games. Games help develop confidence. They help children to learn, to gain factual information, to form a set of basic mental skills, to concentrate, to see relationships and analogies, to be accurate, to form intelligent hypotheses, to follow directions, and to compare and categorize. These skills, learned early in life, will be useful to a person throughout his life.

Another attribute of games is their extreme flexibility. Games can generally be created or adapted to any subject, any kind of problem, or circumstance that may arise. In fact, for those who would intend to use the games that are mentioned on the following pages of this book, I strongly recommend that you begin with a careful evaluation of the content, terminology, and rules of each game that you intend to use. Where your classroom situation would require some adaptation of the game itself, make those adaptations.[9] Use paste-over labels, change the words or pictures, or rewrite the rules. Make whatever other kinds of adjustments are necessary for the game to properly be used as an educational tool within the setting in which you intend to use it.

In addition to the general advantages of games in assisting children to learn, games also help develop specific linguistic skills in ways that may be more conducive to learning for some students than conventional methods. Games help children to learn the skills of definition, the skills of developing his own vocabulary, to learn the various meanings of words, to express his ideas clearly, to identify verbal incongruencies and nuances of meaning, figures of speech and verbal imageries.

It should be noted that games also provide a favorable environment for learning. Children want to play games. Educators for many years have considered games to be "motivational devices".[7] They are a very old and widespread form of learning.[5] It is through the use of games that we can learn the meaning of rules, and that when rules are broken, the game cannot function as originally intended. Although games are one of the most important learning tools available in education today, it is only recently that games have been widely accepted within the field. Historically the earliest games were war games. For example, chess and checkers were devised as games of strategy related to war. Games of more recent years have been used extensively throughout the business world. These so-called management games have been utilized to train executives in problem solving and decision making. Unfortunately, even the word "game" or "games" is considered by many educators as inappropriate for the field of education. Possibly this unenthusiastic response to the use of games in educational settings has been due to differences in the fundamental premises of games and those techniques generally used within the school.

A basic premise of games is that persons do not learn by being taught. They learn by experiencing consequences of their actions. Game devices, activities, and simulations provide for students the opportunity to experience "consequences" before they must experience similar type consequences within real-life situations. Here again, a fundamental difference in premises can be observed. Because of the complexity of life, education tends to departmentalize and selectively teach only certain components of the larger society. Games, on the other hand, are capable of bringing to bear a multiplicity of complex and interrelated elements of the larger society, thereby allowing the students to observe the interplay of those elements within a game situation.

Learning through games has a number of intrinsic virtues. Games, like television, have an attention-focusing quality. They allow students to become actively involved. The use of games deemphasizes the teacher's role as policeman, supervisor, judge, and jury, and allows the teacher to be more of a helper and coach. They allow a student to see the consequences of his actions. A person can recognize more readily that blame for his choices can be placed on no one but himself. He is better able to understand the relationship of his actions to the ultimate outcome.

The degree of chance adds another real-life factor. A properly devised education game must carefully combine the degree of chance with the requirement for an appropriate amount of skill.

Another virtue of games is that they allow children of different abilities to play together without producing segregation that occurs primarily due to their relative degrees of skill. A massive study of the US Office of Education has indicated that children believe that their future depends upon the environment and not on their own efforts.[5] Many disadvantaged children appear to feel a sense of hopelessness toward the formation of their own future. Games can help children to learn that their environment can, to some degree, be predicted and even controlled. Games help children see that their future depends, to a very large extent, directly upon present actions and decision-making skills rather than upon environmental factors alone.

Although some games are designed especially for particular grade levels, we have recently come to understand that games can encompass a wide range of ability levels. A particular game, for example, can be played within an elementary classroom with one set of rules and directions, at the high school or college level with still a different set of directions, and again at a professional level. Although different ability levels may be involved in the playing of a particular game, each level in turn can learn the concepts and the principles inculcated within the game itself.

I can see at least three applications of games to the educational field. Games can be added to an already existing curriculum. They can be utilized within the existing framework of education and in cooperation with existing curriculum materials. Secondly, games can be used as a replacement for quizzes and tests by allowing a child to demonstrate his learning rather than merely repeating back that which he has been taught. A third possibility is to build a curriculum around the use of a comprehensive set of games or around a set of games that encompass much of the complexity of our society. Games can become an important tool in fostering "a sense of self-determination and a capacity for influencing the future."[8]

Some games, such as those described in this book, are for the most part non-competitive in nature. That is to say, one student is not pitted against another, but against the game board itself and the consequences of his own decisions. It is in this fashion that students can practice decision-making techniques.

Besides the fact that "games spur motivation",[4] they are also useful points of departure for discussion. A proper discussion guide developed in conjuction with the concepts of the game itself is very helpful. On this particular issue it must be carefully noted that inexperienced or lazy teachers can abuse the use of games, and that games should not be used in isolation from other curriculum material.

Equally worrisome in many games is the emphasis that is placed on the principle of winning. "It is here that we must be reminded that games should not be over-used to the point that we produce addicts who are more interested in winning than they are in many other important parts of life."[8]

"Games have a remarkable potential for learning."[7] As pointed out in the work of Jean Piaget, "games are more than a caricature of life. They are an introduction to life, an introduction to the idea of rules, an introduction to the idea of playing under different sets of rules, an introduction to the idea of the different roles of life, an introduction to the idea of aiding another person, and an introduction to the idea of working toward a collective goal."[7]

The work of Eric Bryne in the area of transactional analysis and his popular book, *The Games People Play*,[3] has shown us again the close relationship between games and human behavior. Games allow us to be active participants in role-playing situations so that we can experience the different forms of human behavior, and then analyze for ourselves the behavior that we have observed and experienced without becoming committed to a particular course of action or pattern of life.

Games are a simulation of life itself. And yet, paradoxically, they bear a similarity to learning itself, in that learning occurs in successive phases of active participation: learning facts (expressed in terms of the game content), learning processes, and learning the relative cost-benefit, or risk-gain, of alternative strategies. These same successive phases appear to be the content of learning itself in that we first learn the facts, then the processes within which these facts are operative, followed by an understanding of the consequences of the processes involved relative to cost-benefit, gain and loss, and risk/no-risk behavior.

Through the use of games, slower learners appear to learn more from the faster learners than from teachers.

Culturally-deprived students appear to respond better to games than to traditional learning methodology.

Games at their best include a combination of the system sciences and the dramatic arts.

The following games contain a unique design, in that the objective is not winning or losing. The rules of the games and the interaction between players during the course of the games are designed to bring about a greater enhancement of each other. For example, the *Helping Hands* game is designed to introduce the element of sharing positive, constructive, and beneficial gifts with those other players in the game that are less fortunate in their relative position on the game board. Built into the rules of *Timao* is the idea that when a player is unable to formulate an acceptable description of an enhancement or deprivation it is the responsibility of the membership of the game to assist the player in formulating an acceptable response. Similarly, within the directions for *My Cup Runneth Over* there is no penalty involved for guessing. In fact, the process of guessing itself often sparks a beneficial discussion of the rationale behind an interpretation made within the guess.

Educational games are valuable educational tools, particularly as the leader develops more skill in their use. It is with this in mind that I suggest a set of basic steps to be followed in conjuction with the use of games in education.

1. Play the game with a group of adults or children prior to the introduction of the game within the classroom setting.

2. Thoroughly understand the rules with both their limitations and their degrees of freedom.

3. Before you introduce the game, review with the class any words, phrases, or related terminology that may not be clearly understood by the membership of the class.

4. Read carefully the directions for introducing the game as described in the leader's guide, where provided.

5. Recognize that as an educational tool the game does not demand completion. It can be terminated and should be terminated at any point when deemed

appropriate for discussion, for expansion, upon a concept introduced within the game.

6. Utilize to the fullest potential the discussion questions listed in the leader's guide; and with the assistance of the class, develop additional discussion questions.

7. Draw from the class the concepts that they see conveyed within the game, and expand upon that understanding through the use of the list of concepts stated in the leader's guide.

8. Change the wording or adapt the rules wherever necessary due to the age or ability levels of the children involved.

9. It is desirable that during the learning process the basic needs of man be discussed in terms of the original words of the framework (affection, respect, etc.) and learned by the students. These words will become a set of communication "pegs" understood by all members of the group.

10. Games are meant to be fun. Encourage a slow, easy pace in the playing of each game. Allow for an abundance of time during the early stages of learning. To the extent possible, let the students enjoy the pleasure and excitement of the games. Let them laugh a little!

It is through the use of educational games that we begin to utilize to the fullest extent the students' way of viewing things.[1] We gain insights into the perceptions that children hold concerning our world. We become aware of the decisions and the strategies that children see open to them in solving problems. We are able to measure their depth of understanding in a way that cannot be attained through standardized testing.

The games that follow are unique both in their content and in their design. Their content is a presentation of the basic fundamental underlying needs of man. Although they teach facts, factual information is not the goal. Although they communicate and allow children to experience the consequences of their own decisions, learning those consequences is not the goal. The goal of the content presented within the following games is that of laying a foundational basis for the wider shaping and sharing of basic needs. The success or failure of these games should be measured by the degree to which the concepts are practiced by the students.

References

(1) Abt, Clark C., "Games of Learning" in Boocock, Sarane and Schild, E.O., *Simulation Games in Learning,* Beverly Hills: Sage Publications Inc., 1968.

(3) Berne, Eric, *Games People Play,* New York: Grove Press, 1964.

(4) Carlson, Elliot, "Games in the Classroom" in Avedon, Elliot M. and Sutton-Smith, Brian, *The Study of Games,* New York: Wiley, 1971.

(5) Coleman, James S., "Learning through Games," *NEA Journal,* National Education Association, April, 1967.

(7) Hurwitz, Abraham B., and Goodard, Arthur, *Games to Improve Your Child's English,* New York: Simon and Shuster, 1970.

(8) Kraft, Ivor, "Pedagogical Futility in Fun and Games," *NEA Journal,* National Education Association, April, 1967.

(9) Mandel, Murial, *Games to Learn By,* New York: Sterling Publishing Company 1972.

10

VALUE®GAMES

Value®Games provide a non-threatening environment for discussing values. The player will not only learn some basic ideas involved in a value system, but he will develop a foundational awareness of the enhancement and deprivation of values and their relationship to his own life style. He will consciously, or at least subconsciously, recognize that values can be traded through a deliberate transaction. He will learn that a person can transact values with another person or with himself.

He will see that there are enhancements and deprivations of a value even though he may not understand the real meaning of these terms. He will discover that events can be analyzed in terms of the value system. He will also develop some facility in identifying the base values of an event as well as the secondary values.

From this foundational awareness of values the player will sense the usefulness of the value system in the analysis of his own life style. He will begin to see value areas in which he is deprived or overly enhanced. By reviewing the total value system, he will be able to identify areas that should be emphasized to move toward a more satisfying life.

The value framework used in these games was originally developed by Dr. Harold D. Lasswell of Yale University. It appears that this framework can be useful in the analysis of any social or personal aspect of human existence, with a resulting commitment based upon the values.

The Lasswell framework was later refined and related to education by Dr. W. Ray Rucker of United States International University and Dr. V. Clyde Arnspiger of East Texas State University. The games themselves have been developed in cooperation with the author.

The six value games described in this chapter are products of Pennant Educational Materials, San Diego, California. The games generally take 30 to 45 minutes for completion, but play can easily be limited to a set time period.

Value Games are designed to assist the player in developing a basic understanding of concepts involved in a value system. Then, as he becomes conscious of values, he can begin to analyze his own life using values as a base. The games are not intended to produce "winners", but to promote attitudes and activities which will assist the player in understanding how to move toward a more satisfying life.

The BALANCED LIFE in a CRUEL CRUEL WORLD T.M.
Value®Game

PURPOSE

By playing *Cruel Cruel World,* the player begins to develop an understanding of how values are involved in real-life situations. He learns to recognize values and how they are interrelated. This assists him in discovering that events can be interpreted in terms of a value system.

He will realize that his values are enhanced or deprived according to the goals he sets for himself. The player may choose to work for affection, or well-being, or wealth, but he will soon become aware that other values will suffer, and as a result, his limited set of values will not lead him to a balanced life.

The player will discover that a balanced life can only be achieved through balanced values, in terms of the game, eight values. He will learn that this balance can be achieved by transacting values with himself or with another person.

The player will find *Cruel Cruel World* not just a game, but a useful tool for developing skill in analyzing his own life. With this ability he can determine which of his values are being deprived and begin to emphasize these areas to achieve a more satisfying, balanced life.

The game introduces values as players move around the game board. It involves drawing Circumstance cards, Cruel Cruel World cards, and engaging in Transactions with other players or oneself. Some strategy is required, but play is against the board, not in competition with other players. The object is to achieve a balanced life profile on the Enhancement side - a Deprived profile cannot win!

CONCEPTS

It is important that the instructor understand the basic concepts of the *Cruel Cruel World* before play. Listed here are 11 major concepts on which the game is built and the similarity to real-life situations should be noted.

1. There are eight basic value categories: affection, respect, skill, enlightenment, influence, wealth, well-being and responsibility.

2. These values should be balanced, that is, they should be experienced and shared equally.

3. A person can be deprived or enhanced in any value category.

4. Values can be enhanced or deprived through chance or by a planned course of action.

5. A person can become deprived in one value category while simultaneously becoming enhanced in another.

6. It is up to the player to decide how to balance his values.

7. He is able to balance them by himself or through trading with other players.

8. The responsibility of building a balanced life rests with the player, and he will realize that it takes time and planning to achieve this goal.

9. A person needs to re-examine his values continually and to interpret the direction of his life-style.

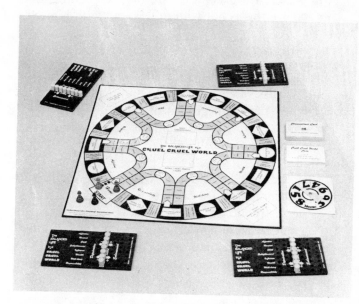

THE BALANCED LIFE IN A CRUEL CRUEL WORLD

For 2 to 4 players or teams. Grade 6 thru Adult.
Game includes 3-color playing surface on large
18"x18" folding game board, 4 scoreboards, 32
scoring pegs, 96 cards, 4 markers, dice (spinner
available on request), instructions, leader's guide.

10. If he concentrates on enhancing one value, others will be deprived as a result.

11. Some may develop a balanced life before others, but the player will become aware that the competition to achieve this is not with others, but with himself.

INTRODUCING THE GAME

The instructor explains that a game is to be played, but does not discuss value categories with the players at this time. Divide them into groups of three or four.

The instructor should remain aware that the mechanics of the game should not supercede the value education.

During the first few minutes of play the instructor should go from group to group to help the students follow the instructions.

This game was designed as a method of helping students discuss values in terms of ordinary experiences. Occasionally the instructor should stop the game for discussion.

It is best to allow players to identify as many concepts as possible from observation before revealing the complete list. During discussion of the concepts, disagreement as well as agreement should be encouraged.

When the students have acquired a basic understanding of the value framework, have the discussions include examples from experiences of their own.

Students can benefit by combining the section of related activities with the playing of the game. This is particularly true in the areas of listing the value categories and defining them, as well as in discussing the meanings and the desirability of a balanced life.

For younger students, it is recommended that the instructions be divided into four sections and read aloud by the instructor.

The first section should include the setting up of the game. Allow the students time to actually set up the game before playing.

Next, instruct the players on where to start, the first five turns, scoring and

Next, instruct the players on where to start, the first five turns, scoring, and the game's end. The students should then begin playing with the instructor going from group to group answering questions.

After a few minutes, the instructor should stop the game and discuss questions which have come up. At that time read instructions which have not already been discussed.

After the students have become acquainted with the game, the teacher should occasionally stop the playing for a short discussion on values.

VARIATIONS OF PLAY

After students have acquired a familiarity with the game, it is possible to vary the circumstances to provide them with a different perspective of the value framework. Some suggestions are as follows:

1. At a predetermined point in the game, scoreboards are traded and playing continues. This can be done once or several times during the game.

2. Have the players stop and analyze their own profile by verbally describing themselves from the position of their scoreboard pegs.

3. Have two persons play as partners by working together on one scoreboard to achieve a balanced value framework.

4. The "Fish Bowl" technique can be very helpful. Adults as well as young people enjoy standing in the outside ring and "Kibitzing" as the four in the inner ring (the fish bowl) are actually playing in the game. After ten or fifteen minutes of play, some members of the outer ring can take the place of the players and go on with the game. This is a happy way for those who feel hesitant to participate at first to feel more at ease. Everyone gets in on the excitement!

DISCUSSION QUESTIONS

The following questions are illustrative of the type of questions that could be profitably utilized before, during, and after the playing of *The Balanced Life in a Cruel Cruel World.* Since a range of ability levels are exposed to the game, it is important that the teacher or group leader rephrase questions to meet the level of understanding of the participants.

1. What is a balanced life?

2. Do you feel that the game's definition of a balanced life is valid? Why? (Or why not?)

3. How do your definitions of each of the eight value areas compare to the word examples listed within each value loop on the game board?

4. If you concentrate on enhancing only one value area, what are the effects upon other value areas?

5. What examples can you give of enhancement and/or deprivation as the result of chance?

6. What examples can you give of enhancement and/or deprivation as the result of a planned course of action?

7. What are the differences between the game rules and real life circumstances related to transactions?

*MY CUP RUNNETH OVER*_{T.M.}
Value_® Game

PURPOSE

The essential purpose of *My Cup Runneth Over* is to assist the player in communicating his values and interpreting the values communicated by others. He will become aware of how values are expressed in words, actions and in combination of both words and actions.

The player will begin to realize that his values are interpreted differently by other players, and how he sees himself is often not the way they see him. He will learn that communicating his values accurately to others takes time and practice on his part. By playing *My Cup Runneth Over*, the player becomes aware of how to recognize values which are being communicated to him, and will begin to apply this ability, thereby developing a better understanding of himself and others.

The game involves non-programmed role playing. Successful interpretation of the value being portrayed enables players to fill their cups. Players engage in active interpersonal exchange while helping one another to achieve.

CONCEPTS

Before introducing the game to players, it is recommended that the instructor become familiar with the eight basic concepts of the game, and their relation to real life.

1. There are eight basic value categories: affection, respect, skill, enlightenment, influence, wealth, well-being, and responsibility.

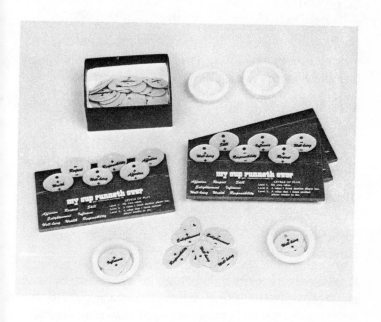

MY CUP RUNNETH OVER

For 2 to 4 players or teams. Grade 6 thru Adult.
Game includes "Well" for tokens during play, 4
display racks, 4 cups, 80 hot-stamped plastic tokens,
instructions, leader's guide.

2. Values can be expressed or communicated in words, actions and in combinations of words and actions.

3. We understand others by how they communicate their values.

4. People vary in their ability to express their values and in interpreting values communicated by others.

5. Expressing and interpreting values are skills which can be improved.

6. Others see us as seeking or possessing certain values, and these values can be accidently enhanced or deprived by chance.

7. Values can be deliberately enhanced through self-effort.

8. Values can be deliberately deprived through neglect.

INTRODUCING THE GAME

It is highly recommended that the instructor become familiar with the game before introducing it to the students. A suggested method would be to play the game with other instructors in an atmosphere similar to that of a teachers' lounge.

The instructor should not discuss value concepts with the students prior to the game, but should remain aware that *My Cup Runneth Over* is a stepping-stone to a meaningful discussion of values.

Students should be divided into groups of three or four and the rules read aloud by the instructor. For younger students, refer to the section introducing them to the *Cruel Cruel World.*

A typical game could proceed as follows:

A student, after selecting six chips would place, for example, (-) wealth in front of his board face down. He would say, "I am playing my own value (level one). My bike had a flat yesterday, so I had to buy a new tube and tire."

The other students would place face down in front of their boards a chip representing the value they think he is portraying.

The chips are turned up and if any match (-) wealth, those chips would be deposited in each individual's cup. Chips not matching would be deposited in the "well", then all players would select one more chip from the "well".

If no players felt they could have matched the actor's message, then each could have verbally guessed. All who guessed (-) wealth could have drawn a chip from the "well" and placed it in their cups.

If a player had correctly guessed the message, and had played two (-) wealth chips, both chips would be put in his cup and he would draw two more from the "well." The actor could also have played two (-) wealth chips if he had them in his rack at the beginning of play.

Using multiple messages is not recommended until the players become familiar with the game. An example could be "I am playing two of my own values (level one). My bike had a flat yesterday, so I had to buy a new tube and tire. This was the first time I had repaired a bicycle tire, so I learned something." The chips he played could have been (-) wealth and (+) skill.

Other examples could be:

(-) responsibility (level three) "I know you are afraid to lend me your car because I scraped the fender last time."

(+) enlightenment (level two) "I noticed when I came over to your house last night you were reading. It seems that everytime I see you, you are reading something."

(-) affection (level one) "My girl friend broke up with me last night because I hardly ever walk her home from school."

(+) well-being (level one) "I did the shopping for my mother last night, and although I missed a basketball game, it made me feel pretty good just to help her out."

VARIATIONS OF PLAY

1. Play the game by acting out the role of another person such as an Indian living on a reservation, or as a black man in the ghetto, or as a historical person such as Lincoln. A black man in the ghetto might, for example, consider (+) responsibility as finding a job, and (-) wealth in having his rent raised. Lincoln might have considered his 10-mile walk to return a book a (-) in well-being and a (+) in respect.

2. In a large group, have students take turns coming up to the front of the class and drawing a chip. The person would then act out the value written on the chip while the class guesses which value he is expressing. The class can be divided into teams and a record of scores kept.

3. Pass out a chip to everyone in the class. Have each person express the value on his chip while the others write down what they think it is. The object is to see who can get the most correct answers. Someone will be needed to keep track of correct answers in order to check the students' responses.

4. Require the students to give true illustrations from their own lives rather than creating illustrations only for game purposes.

DISCUSSION QUESTIONS

The following questions are illustrative of the type of questions that could be profitably utilized before, during, and after the playing of *My Cup Runneth Over*. Since a range of ability levels are exposed to the game, it is important that the teacher or group leader rephrase questions to meet the understanding of the participants.

1. What are some examples of a value category expressed or communicated in words only?

2. What are some examples of a value category expressed or communicated in action without words?

3. What are some examples of a value category expressed or communicated in words as an enhancement and in action as a deprivation?

4. What are some examples of a value category expressed or communicated in words as a deprivation and in action as an enhancement?

5. How can we improve our ability to express the value category intended in our words and actions?

6. How can we improve our ability to interpret the values expressed by others?

7. What are some examples of the deprivation of others through a neglect of sharing or communication?

TIMAO T.M.
Value ® Game

PURPOSE

Timao is designed to assist the player in understanding that events are multi-valued and any event may involve both the enhancement and deprivation of values.

The player will become aware that the ability to see and express values is important in both self-analysis and in understanding others.

He will develop the ability to view events in relationship to several values, and discover that these values are interrelated.

The game involves verbal identification of values. Players may describe their own real-life experiences or role-play real or imaginary situations to play out the value area cards.

CONCEPTS

The instructor should understand the relationship between *Timao* and real-life situations. Because of this, seven major concepts have been included here, and the instructor should become familiar with them before presenting the game to other players.

1. There are eight basic value categories: responsibility, well-being, respect, skill, enlightenment, influence, affection and wealth.

2. Values are deprived or enhanced in everyday situations, and several values may be involved in a single event.

3. An event may cause the deprivation of some values and simultaneously the enhancement of others.

4. Values are expressed or communicated in words and actions, and people may recognize different values in the same event.

5. People vary in their ability to express and interpret the values involved in a situation, but they can develop this ability and acquire a better understanding of values.

6. This ability can come about by accident or by gaining skill through practice.

7. Becoming aware of value concepts can be a means of self-analysis and can assist in understanding others.

INTRODUCING THE GAME

The instructor should remain aware that the discussion of value categories should not begin until after the players have played the game and become familiar with its mechanics. The instructor should divide the class into groups of three to five, and read the directions aloud. A typical game could go as follows:

Player A, after receiving his eight cards, turns an event card over which says "Paid a Bill." He lays a (-) wealth card next to the value card and says,

"I paid my phone bill today. It was $18.00."

Player B lays a (+) influence card next to the other two cards and says,

"My bank is impressed that I always pay my bills on time so I am able to get that loan I wanted."

Player C lays a (-) affection card down and says,

"It was my girl friend's birthday yesterday, but since I paid my phone bill, I didn't have enough money to buy her a present, so I lost a little affection."

Player A puts down a (+) respect card and says,

TIMAO

For 2 to 5 players. Grade 6 thru Adult.
Game includes 48 value cards, 20 event cards,
instructions, leader's guide.

"Although I couldn't buy her a present, she respects me more because I paid my bill on time."

Player B cannot play a card so he draws another. The card he draws he is unable to play so he says "Pass."

Player C says "I felt good paying the bill on time. I gained a little well-being." And he lays down a (+) well-being card.

The game continues until eight cards have been played. The last person to play a card receives the event card and shuffles the eight value cards back into the deck.

VARIATIONS OF PLAY

1. Have a player draw a card and read the situation. Other players would then raise their hands and suggest values involved and someone could list them on the board. After the group develops skill, a time limit could be used. Teams could compete to see who could get all eight value categories on a situation in the shortest time.

2. Make up new phrase cards which apply more specifically to the group or persons playing. These cards can be used in the above activity or in the *Timao* game.

3. This variation is much more challenging and some of the ideas, such as using only three cards, may be incorporated permanently into the playing of the game. Use this variation only after the students have become familiar with the basic method of playing. Deal three *Timao* cards face down to each player and one card face up next to the event card. The first player begins story using the *Timao* card face up near

the event card. He then places one of his *Timao* cards face up and the next person continues the story. The second player places another *Timao* card down to which the third player would relate the story, and so on. The person who plays the eighth card finishes the story. It may be that he had also told the story for the seventh card. The person who plays the eighth card collects the event card and reshuffles the eight *Timao* cards into the deck.

DISCUSSION QUESTIONS

The following questions are illustrative of the type of questions that could be profitably utilized before, during, and after the playing of Timao. Since a range of ability levels are exposed to the game, it is important that the teacher or group leader rephrase questions to meet the understanding of the participants.

1. What are your definitions of each of the eight value areas?

2. What are the examples of deprivation and enhancement (losses and gains) in each of the value areas?

3. Does chance or planning play the greater role in the balance of values?

4. What are some examples of situations in which one or more value categories were enhanced and simultaneously produced deprivations in other categories?

5. What are some examples of situations in which an enhancement and deprivation could occur within the same value area?

113

6. Have there been any situations in your own life which less than four value areas were involved?

7. What are some situations in which several (at least three) different interpretations of the possible value eι hancements and deprivations can be given?

HELPING HANDS_{T.M.}
Play-By-Colors
Value® Game

Pre-School through Third Grade

PURPOSE

Helping Hands is a game for two to six players designed for pre-school and primary level non-readers and readers. Players are introduced to eight value areas along a road around the playing surface. Each move is determined by drawing a *Helping Hands* card. The players have opportunities to "help" other players to advance. The sharing of values and caring for others are the two central learning experiences in the game.

The purpose of the game is to communicate an awareness of values through the process of play and to strengthen the concept of sharing with others from the storehouse of each one's own value enhancements.

CONCEPTS

Helping Hands provides an environment for relating some important concepts to real-life situations. The major concepts found in the game are listed below. The players will become somewhat familiar with them during play. The teacher, however, may wish to deepen this understanding through related exercises or discussion before, during or after play.

1. There are eight value areas: responsibility, well-being, respect, skill, enlightenment, influence, affection, wealth.

2. All value areas are equal in importance.

3. There are times when one person can help another person.

4. One person may have more opportunities to be helpful than another.

5. By circumstance (the draw of a card in the case of this game) a person may be deprived (-) or enhanced (+) in a value area.

6. An enhanced person is more able to help another person.

7. There are intrinsic gains of happiness when one person shares with another.

8. Values can be shared.

9. Sharing does not mean a loss to yourself.

10. Another person can be helped in any of the eight value categories.

INTRODUCING THE GAME (Basic Instructions)

Shuffle the deck of *Helping Hands* cards. Place the cards face down on the board in the large *Helping Hands* title area. Each player selects a marker and places it on Start.

The players decide who will take the first turn. Each in turn draws the top card and lays it face up in a pile next to the deck. If he draws a plus (+) card, he moves forward to the next space which is the same color as the card. If he draws a minus (-) card, he moves backward to the same color as the card.

Whenever a player moves his marker PAST a *Helping Hands* space, he helps the player whose marker is last in line by moving that player's marker to the next *Helping Hands* space.

HELPING HANDS

For 2 to 6 players. Grades K-3.
Game includes 8-color playing surface on large 18"x18" folding game board, 32 cards in colors which match squares on playing board, 6 markers, instructions, leader's guide.

When the first player reaches the home area, the game is over. When a player draws a card of a color which is not on the board between his position and "Home", he goes "Home".

VARIATION OF PLAY

Players, as they become able to interpret the pictures or read the value categories on the cards, should begin to use the value categories as a way to explain why it is possible to help another player.

DISCUSSION QUESTIONS

The following questions are meant to be illustrative of the type of questions that can be used with the *Helping Hands* game. Differences in ability levels may require that the teacher rephrase the questions.

1. How many different colors are there in the game?

2. What do the pictures on the cards show?

3. What are the words on the cards that can be used to describe the pictures on the cards?

4. Does everyone in the world have chances to help someone? Explain.

5. What are the ways you can help someone today? Give examples.

6. How do you feel when you help someone?

7. How do you think the person you helped feels?

MATCH WITS™
Value® Game

Game moves fast, excitement builds while racing the timer. *MATCH WITS* develops an understanding of the possible needs and wants expressed in typical human situations. Involves team play, 1 to 5 per team, with participation by each of the players.

PURPOSE

To develop an understanding of the possible value needs and wants behind the behavior expressed in human situations. To develop ability in the analysis of these common situations. To strengthen and broaden the understanding of potential value gains and losses that can be perceived in human interaction.

To develop a foundational awareness of the range of possible behaviors and attitudes that reflect the withholding of value needs and the sharing and enhancement of value needs. To develop insight into the value-laden characteristics of every deliberate act of man.

CONCEPTS

. There are eight basic value categories: *responsibility, well-being, respect, skill, enlightenment, influence, affection and wealth.*

. Values are deprived or enhanced in everyday situations, and several values may be involved in a single event.

. An event may cause the deprivation of some values and simultaneously the enhancement of others.

119

4. Becoming aware of value concepts can be a means of self-analysis and can assist in understanding others.

5. A group can cooperate in recognizing the deprivations and enhancements in a situation.

6. All eight value areas can be recognized in a situation.

7. People can learn to recognize and give explanations of a variety of possible value enhancements and deprivations in a given situation.

8. One can see enhancements even in a seemingly negative situation.

9. One can see deprivations in a seemingly positive situation.

INTRODUCING THE GAME

Divide the large group into smaller groups of no more than 10 persons per group. Each small group divided into two teams needs one score sheet, one timer, and one set of situation cards. The situation cards are shuffled and placed face down. Two score keepers and a time keeper are selected.

The game begins when the first situation card is turned face up and read aloud and the timer is started. Team A has one minute to indicate possible enhancements in the value areas as a result of the stated situation. When one minute has elapsed, the tally marks are added together. Team B then has one minute to state the deprivations that might result in the same situation.

The second part of Round 1 continues with the reading of the second situation card. Team B gives the possible enhancements and Team A the deprivations. The score is derived by subtracting the deprivation sub

MATCH WITS

For 2 to 40 players. Grades 4 thru Adult.
Game includes 64 situation cards, 100 score cards, 4
timers, instructions, leader's guide.

total from the enhancement sub-total. After all four rounds have been completed (or an earlier point if desired), the points for all rounds are added together. The team with the highest score wins the game.

DISCUSSION QUESTIONS

1. What example of an unpleasant situation can you give that has enhancement possibilities?

2. What example of a pleasant situation can you give that could cause the deprivation of values as well as enhancement?

3. What example can you give of a situation that was both a deprivation and an enhancement?

4. How does it help to work together with other people to analyze situations?

5. Give an example of a situation in your own life. In how many value areas could you have been enhanced? In how many value areas could you have been deprived in that same situation?

6. What is a deprivation?

7. What is an enhancement?

VALUE BINGO T.M.
Value® Game

A 25-square adaptation of the familiar Bingo game. Players have fun interpreting statements and positioning their markers accordingly. Verification of the correct response follows each play, allowing immediate self-check.

Develops an awareness of the primary value category which may be involved in a situation. Provides plenty of opportunity for discussion at the classroom level.

PURPOSE

Players learn to interpret verbal statements in terms of underlying value intent. They learn to freely evaluate each statement since there is no penalty for guessing and the "correct" answer is provided after each statement is read. Ability to differentiate between enhancement and deprivational statements is quickly developed. Opportunity for discussion at the classroom level is provided.

INTRODUCING THE GAME

Since the majority of students are familiar with the way to play the usual game of Bingo, the only introduction needed is the identification of the abbreviations used in the Value Bingo card squares and the significance of the positive (+) and negative (-) symbols.

A = *Affection*

E = *Enlightenment*

I = *Influence*

R = *Respect*

Ry = *Responsibility*

S = *Skill*

W = *Wealth*

W B = *Well-being*

Each player takes a Value Bingo card and 20 to 25 tokens. The leader mixes the statement cards and places them face down in the box.

He draws a statement card and reads the statement printed on its face. 15 to 30 seconds are allowed for players to interpret the statement and to place a token on the Value Bingo card. (Gray side up.)

The leader then reads the value category printed on the statement card and puts a token on the space for that category on the master card. Players who do not have the same answer as the statement card are to reposition their tokens on the correct answer.

All players then turn the last played token over (red side up).

Continue play, reading statements and positioning tokens, until some player gets 5 tokens in a row, any direction.

CONCEPTS

1. There are eight value categories.
2. There are positive and negative sides to each value category.

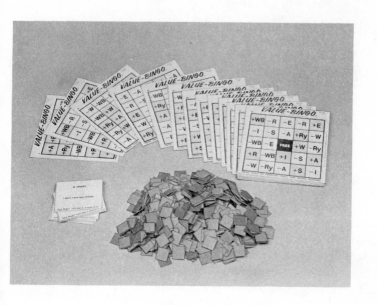

VALUE BINGO®

For 2 to 40 players. Grades 4 thru Adult.

Game includes 40 different Value Bingo cards, approximately 800 playing tokens, 32 situation cards, master card, instructions, leader's guide.

125

3. Each value area can be understood in everyday terms and experiences.

4. In each experience or statement one value area is emphasized or stands out.

5. A person can learn to recognize the value area involved in these representative experiences and statements.

PRINCIPLES (To be used in the development of new statements.)

1. In each statement the player is to be the recipient of the action, or the possessor of the value described. (Two levels: things which he receives; things which he possesses.)

2. The statements are to be non-threatening in teacher-pupil relationships, or in pupil-pupil relationships.

3. Only enhancing words are to be used. On the negative side, enhancing words are combined with negative modifiers.

4. The statements are to include synonyms for the value categories involved, and are to be kept purposely simple for ease in identifying the base value being described.

5. There are to be two enhancement statements and two deprivation statements for each value category.

DISCUSSION QUESTIONS

1. What are the eight value areas represented in this game?

2. What synonyms can you give for each value area?

3. What statements or experiences can you give other than those in the game which might also illustrate each value on the deprivation and the enhancement side?

4. What did you do this week that shows enhancement in responsibility?

5. What have you done to show respect for others or earn respect from self or others today?

6. What happened to make you feel good today?

7. What decisions did you make today?

11

RELATED ACTIVITIES

For Understanding The Inter-Relationship of The Eight Value Areas

GROUP ACTIVITIES

The following activities are designed to increase the student's understanding of the eight value areas, and how the value areas are related to events, to other persons and to the student himself.

1. Have someone write on the chalkboard the list of students' wants and needs. Then make a list across the board of the eight value areas. Try and put items from the wants and needs list under the proper value area headings. Discuss the relationship between the two lists.

2. To help learn names of the value areas, go around the group having the first person name one area. The next person would name that area and add another until all eight are named. The purpose is to see how many people are needed to name all eight without repeating a value or skipping a player. Attempt to cut down on the number of times, until it requires only eight people to name the areas without error. Start with a different player each time you play.

3. Think of words which fit into each value area, and discuss the definition of these words.

4. Discuss or write down examples of events in which a value is enhanced or deprived.

5. Give examples of how a person can be deprived in one value area with a resulting enhancement in another.

6. Develop a bulletin board of value areas. Students can bring pictures to put under the various area headings.

7. Make up a dictionary of values. Have definitions of each value area in students' own words. Add pictures or examples if possible.

8. Book reports can be written in terms of values. Characters or events in the story can be discussed in relationship to values enhanced or deprived.

9. Have students give examples of being enhanced or deprived, and how they may have enhanced or deprived others during the school day. After recess or toward the end of the day are suggested times for this activity.

10. List subjects studied in class and have students explain which values are enhanced or deprived by learning or not learning each subject.

11. Name a famous person who has deprived himself in one value area in order to be enhanced in some other value area.

12. Discuss a problem situation in personal relationships in class in terms of values deprived and enhanced.

13. Analyze the values of a television program, news event, cartoon, personal experience, famous person, etc. Notice which values are used in commercials to influence the listeners.

14. Write anecdotes or short stories to illustrate enhancement or deprivation of a value or to illustrate a value-sharing situation.

15. Suggest other possible value areas and discuss whether they are included in the eight Lasswell value areas.

16. For the next several weeks, make a notebook of newspapers or magazine articles which clearly highlight the value areas. Try to get both a positive and a negative emphasis. In a few words, state clearly how the article is related to the value area.

CREATIVE WRITING IDEAS

After the students have acquired a basic understanding of what values are, it is suggested that they write a composition or give an extemporaneous speech on experiences, goals and outlooks in terms of the value areas. This will enable the student to reflect upon himself and his actions in relationship to his value framework, and will assist him in becoming aware of the practical application of the value framework to his own life.

The following are some suggested subject areas:

1. If I Could Do Anything I Wanted....
2. When I Grow Up....
3. I Enjoy My Family Most When We....
4. I Wish I Had More Time To....
5. One Thing I Would Like to Change is....
6. My Feelings get Hurt When....
7. What Makes Me Mad....
8. What Makes Me Sad....
9. What Makes Me Happy....
10. A Well-Rounded Person is Multi-Valued.
11. Who Am I?
12. What I Like About Myself....
13. It Makes Me Angry When....
14. I Would Like to be President....
15. Why Do I Go On Living Each Day?
16. What Things Are Important To Me?

SONGS EMPHASIZING VALUES

The following is a partial list of songs emphasizing values. The songs will assist the younger students in relating values to concepts with which they are familiar. After singing, the songs' interpretations may be seen from a different perspective as the students discuss them using terms and ideas learned from playing the value games. The instructor and students may wish to select other songs for similar use.

Affection:
  Polly-Wolly-Doodle
  Red River Valley
  Auld Lang Syne

Respect:
  For He's a Jolly Good Fellow
  The Star Spangled Banner
  It's a Small World

Skill:
  The Man on the Flying Trapeze
  Humpty Dumpty
  Pat-A-Cake
  Mary, Mary, Quite Contrary

Enlightenment:
  When You Wish Upon a Star
  Twinkle Twinkle Little Star
  The Bear Went Over the Mountain

Influence:
  I'd Like To Teach The World To Sing
  Little Miss Muffet
  Who's Afraid of the Big Bad Wolf

Wealth:
  America the Beautiful
  Old McDonald Had a Farm
  Simple Simon

Well-Being:
  Funiculi, Funicula
  Home On The Range
  Oh Susanna
  When You're Smiling

Responsibility:
  I've Been Working on the Railroad
  Old McDonald Had a Farm
  Sweet and Low
  Little Boy Blue

The following are some examples of worksheets for students.

"SUPER GOOD" CHART

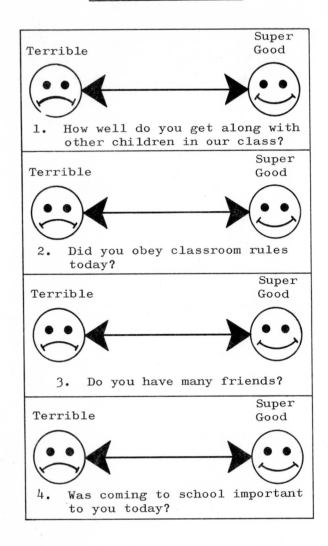

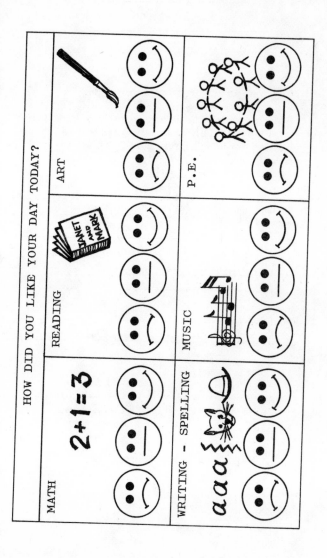

FAMOUS PEOPLE

Instructions:

A. Beside each famous person, list the achievements for which he (she) is most noted and the values you believe motivated those achievements. Example:

	ACHIEVEMENTS	VALUES
Cortez	_____	_____
	_____	_____
Lincoln	_____	_____
	_____	_____
Henry Ford	_____	_____
	_____	_____

B. Discuss the value system which guided each person's actions. Were his values respect by his society? How would he be accepted if he were alive today?

VALUING MYSELF

Instructions:

Divide a piece of paper into four squares. Repeat the process for a second piece of paper. List one of the eight value areas on the bottom of each square. In each square draw a picture that shows how you would value yourself in that value area. Example:

(Picture of me combing my hair) AFFECTION	(Picture of me looking at myself in a mirror) RESPECT
(Picture of me learning to skate) SKILL	(Picture of me reading a book) ENLIGHTENMENT

BECOMING AWARE OF VALUES

VALUING OTHERS

Instructions:

Divide a piece of paper into four squares. Repeat the process for a second piece of paper. List one of the eight value areas on the bottom of each square. In each square draw a picture of how you would share the value with others.

(Picture of me voting) INFLUENCE	(Picture of me giving to a poor man) WEALTH
(Picture of me teaching someone how to run a race) WELL-BEING	(Picture of me helping someone across the street) RESPONSIBILITY

VALUE RELATIONS

Instructions:

Listed below are a group of words for which you are to find both a synonym and antonym. Use your dictionary if necessary, but try to do it on your own first.

Value Word	Synonym	Antonym
affection		
respect		
skill		
enlightenment		
influence		
wealth		
well-being		
responsibility		
friendship		
honor		
talent		
knowledge		
leadership		
services		
health		
happiness		
justice		

9th GRADE ENGLISH ASSIGNMENT:

THE SWORD IN THE STONE

Directions: Write full answers, not one word answers.

1. The governess who was the boy's teacher failed to punish Kay for errors. Again when the boys went hunting Kay was never "bladed" for errors as was the rule for others. Which of the human values (needs) was being weakened for Kay?

2. What did he do at almost the end of the book that showed this weakness (deprivation), even though he later confessed when confronted with the necessity of demonstrating the feat? Did this make you like him better or less? Why?

3. Which values were continually re-inforced for both boys by those responsible for them?

4. What did this do for their development toward their futures?

5. In which values was Kay superior to Wart? How did these advantages effect Kay? How did they effect Wart?

6. When did you first know in reading the book that Wart was perhaps intended for a different future than just being the squire of Kay?

7. How had Wart become a member of Sir Ector's family?

8. Show how each of Wart's adventures were responsible for Wart's final triumph when he fulfilled the prophesy and proved himself the rightful King of England.

9. How would these same accomplishments re-inforce a candidate for the presidency of the United States?

10. What was the final task that Wart performed?

11. Can you relate the re-inforcements Wart enjoyed to your own life?

Example of 9th grade English student's response:

1. *Kay was deprived of respect because he lost the respect for other people (he became contemptous of their permissiveness), rectitude*

because if he was never corrected for doing something wrong, how would he know if he was really right or wrong, enlightenment for not knowing (or learning) what's right or wrong.

2. *When Wart showed him the sword from the stone, Kay told his father that he pulled it out. No, it did not make me like him better because he shouldn't have done it in the first place, but at least he told the truth after his father questioned him.*

3. *They re-inforced affection for Wart and Kay, Wart had it, but I don't think Kay did. Wart had respect for everyone and everything, but Kay didn't really have it. Well-being, Wart and Kay had physical, mental, emotional abilities; Rectitude, Wart had a sense of right and wrong, Kay did but not as much as Wart. Enlightenment, Wart had really gained his knowledge from experience and reading, Kay mostly from reading. Wart learned to cherish the valuable things such as love, understanding, etc. Skill, just physical means.*

4. *Wart— learned to care for others (affection) and to understand people, to train better (skill), to hold his temper better (respect) and become more of a man (self respect). Kay didn't learn or know as much as Wart about human needs and wants (values), because he was deprived of discipline so Wart turned out more sharing and enhanced or "better".*

5. *The values, knowledge and practiced sharing that made Kay feel superior to Wart were wellbeing and power because Kay was to become a knight and Wart couldn't. Kay had a father and mother and Wart didn't, which greatly affected his affection, respect and rectitude (as well as well-being). It also had to have important effects on his skill and enlightenment. Kay teased Wart about this increasing sense of power but made Kay feel superior and Wart inferior which deprived him of power.*

6. *When Merylyn came along and gave Wart more adventures than Kay.*

7. *Merylyn had taken Wart away from his own family and sort of put him on the doorstep which made it possible for him to get higher position (wealth, affection, respect, etc.).*

8. *From all these adventures Wart learned the knowledge of how to be a man and skill of being thoughtful and thankful — sharing and receiving skill, respect, affection, enlightenment, power, and rectitude).*

9. *It would help them understand, and care for people, to love and respect themselves and others, and become enlightened about other people, their needs and wants.*

10. *When Wart proved his worth and pulled the sword out and became King Arthur.*

11. *I enjoy affection for other people, respect for myself and other people, wellbeing of physical, mental, emotional enjoyment, rectitude, enlightenment, power, wealth, skill. I get these from my parents, friends, school and places where I go.*

— Used by permission of Garnet Brayer

VALUE DOMINOES

tructions:

Make a set of word cards like a domino set.
set should contain 16 different word groups,
. +affection; -affection; +respect; -respect,
. Make up from copies of each word group.
word groups are used on each card with a few
bles. The game is played just like dominoes.

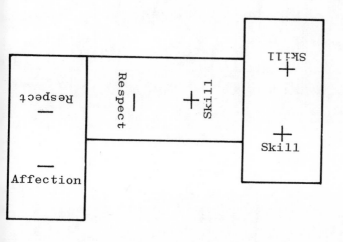

VALUE WORD SEARCH

Instructions:

Look for the words listed below in the squa
of letters. They are in straight lines and don'
skip any letters. You may find a word by readin
up, down, forward, backward, or diagonally.

Draw a circle around the words as you find
them, and cross them off the list. The words do
not use all the letters in the puzzle, but some
letters are used more than once.

A	W	F	J	A	D	M	I	R	A	T	I	O	N	B
T	A	K	C	C	T	N	O	Z	Q	P	M	F	G	F
T	R	C	A	R	D	E	N	T	B	A	Q	A	A	A
R	M	O	R	T	R	U	S	O	T	S	Z	S	C	M
A	H	N	I	L	J	K	T	R	U	S	T	C	C	I
C	E	F	N	T	W	L	A	R	A	I	K	I	E	L
T	A	I	G	Z	E	T	P	F	Q	O	N	N	P	I
I	R	D	P	L	L	N	A	R	J	N	M	A	T	A
V	T	E	G	I	C	Z	D	I	J	Z	N	T	A	R
E	E	N	J	K	O	O	X	E	O	O	P	I	N	I
N	D	C	L	I	M	X	R	N	R	E	K	O	C	T
E	Z	E	O	N	E	A	T	D	T	N	Z	N	E	Y
S	T	N	V	G	V	W	P	L	I	K	E	O	Z	T
S	Q	O	E	F	A	N	C	Y	Z	A	J	S	T	P
I	N	T	I	M	A	C	Y	V	R	E	L	Y	S	A

1. ATTRACTIVENESS
2. CARING
3. LIKING
4. FANCY
5. TRUST
6. CONFIDENCE
7. RELY
8. TENDERNESS
9. ACCEPTANCE
10. FASCINATION
11. INTIMACY
12. FAMILIARITY
13. FRIENDLY
14. ARDENT
15. CORDIAL
16. WARM-HEARTED
17. WELCOME
18. LOVE
19. ADMIRATION
20. PASSION

Other "Word Search" suggestions that can be used.

1. Words that relate to value areas found in a story being read. (Kissed, hugged, friendly, scared, etc.)

2. Objects that relate to a value area. (Respect, trophy, badge, title, uniform, etc.)

3. Things that we love. (Mother, baby, toys, bike, friends, etc.)

4. Things that we respect. (Country, flag, laws, rules, parents, God, etc.)

5. Things that require skill. (Art, music, sports, teaching, climbing, etc.)

6. Things that require enlightenment. (Teaching, reading, writing, speaking, etc.)

7. Things that relate to power. (Leaders, principals, guns, etc.)

8. Things that relate to wealth. (Money, property, food, TV, clothes, etc.)

9. Things that relate to well-being. (Health, happiness, strength, joy, peace, etc.)

10. Things that relate to responsibility. (Promises, trust, fairness, justice, etc.)

11. Enhancements toward self. (Sleep, eat, exercise, read, etc.)

12. Enhancements toward others. (Smile, praise, share, teach, give, etc.)

13. Enhancements from others. (Recognition, gifts, services, protection, etc.)

14. Make a collage of things rather than a word list.

15. Positive or enhancing reply words. (Thanks, welcome, sorry, pardon, etc.)

16. Make a word list in which the opposite word is in the square of letters. (Hate (love), friend (foe), good (bad), etc.)

17. Have a square of letters but no word list. The directions would have you find certain types of words and write the word list. (Good things to have, depriving words, enhancing words, etc.)

VALUE LACING

Instructions:

Cards with pictures on the left side, and related words, sentences, or paragraphs on the right side. Make the cards so that the pictures and their related phrases are not across from each other. The children can join the matching items with shoe laces or cord.

(Add picture of person sweeping) ⬤   How to be a helper ⭕

(Picture) ⭕   Sweep the floor ⬤

(Picture) ⭕   Pick up things   ⭕

(Picture) ⭕   Share a book   ⭕

(Picture) ⭕   Visit a friend   ⭕

(Picture) ⭕   Give a gift   ⭕

147

WORD ASSOCIATION GAME

Pick one of the value category names or a synonym as an <u>ending</u> word to a list.

<u>Start</u> with any word you want. (This could be an oral or written project.) Make a list of words with each word related to only the word before it. Keep going until the desired value word is reached. <u>EXAMPLE</u>:

<u>Wealth</u>	<u>Affection</u>
scissors	cup
cut	drink
cake	water
birthday	wet
presents	hose
wealth	faucet
	turn
	game
	play
	friends
	like
	affection

LETTER WRITING

Each child makes a mailbox out of a milk
carton -- cut tops off of cartons and cover with
contact paper. Put a strip of masking tape in
each box with the child's name on it. Staple the
boxes together. Add your own box (with teacher's
name) to the set.

Making mailboxes, writing letters or notes,
and also receiving letters bring in many values
for the child. Set aside a day for each of the
following:

- Writing someone a note that you like them and
tell why.
- Writing someone a note that you respect them
and tell why.
- Writing someone a note that you recognize their
skills and tell why.
  Writing someone a note that you recognize their
enlightenment and tell why.
  Writing someone a note that you recognize their
influence and tell why.
  Writing someone a note that you recognize their
wealth and tell why.
  Writing someone a note that you recognize their
well-being and tell why.
  Writing someone a note that you recognize their
responsibility and tell why.

All notes may be signed or unsigned. All must
positive.

(NOTE: Occasionally some child will not
receive a letter. In this case, the teacher may
wish to write a letter to the child, or even better,
other children will notice this lack and take steps
their own to write him a letter.)

RELATED WORDS

Instructions:

Give each child a piece of grid paper with a copy of words related to a value area. Have them individually or in small groups devise a li of related words similar to the examples listed below:

								I								
	E	N	L	I	G	H	T	E	N	M	E	N	T			
			E					Q								
			A					U								
			R				D	I	S	C	O	V	E	R		
	F	I	N	D	O	U	T		R							
							R	E	A	L	I	Z	E			
						A										
						B										
						I										
			S	K	I	L	L									
						I										
						T	A	L	E	N	T					
						Y										

12

CHAPTER 12

AFFECTION

Activities Related to Understanding the Affection Value Area

DEFINITION: *Love and friendship that you have for other people and that you feel they have or should have for you.*

DESCRIPTIVE BEHAVIORS: *Those behaviors that affect the way you feel about yourself and others in the areas of receiving and providing emotional security, love, congeniality and friendship.*

BEHAVIORAL OBJECTIVES (Principal Value Goals): *Acceptance, trust, emotional security, love, congeniality and friendliness.*

The following activities are designed to increase the student's understanding of the *affection* value area. Where feasible, an activity should include not only some discussion of the activity. but also. more importantly, its application to the student's own life. While the activities as presented range from early elementary through adult

level, most can be adapted to suit the age or comprehension of a particular group of students.

1. Ask some adults if there are any groups they belong to now or in the past to which they feel affection.

2. Tell in what ways we demonstrate a feeling of affection for our class as a whole. How does the teacher give and receive affection.

3. Classify happenings in history as to main value categories.

4. Make a class picture book showing adults at work in different occupations.

5. Have a Conference Time at a specific time each day — maybe only for ten minutes. Children can sign up to have a conference, or special time to talk to you all by themselves at that time.

6. Have a "Friendship Corner" where children who are having a disagreement go to iron out the problems. When the matter is settled, they rejoin the class.

7. Make scrapbook of neighborhood friends. (Get autograph, hobby, where born, where they work, why you like them.)

8. Read story such as Huckleberry Finn and discuss relationships to value areas.

9. Write and illustrate a class book or experience chart titled, "What is a Friend?" or "How Do I Choose a Friend?"

10. Read the *Boy Who Called Wolf.* Discuss the moral of the story. Discuss the idea that people who consistently deprive others of respect may find their affection rejected.

11. Make a chart story telling what friends can do for each other.

12. Devise with class a welcoming system for new students.

13. Make something for a friend as a demonstration of affection.

14. Have a "secret pal" for a week. Do nice things for him or her.

**The following are some examples
of worksheets for students.**

LITERATURE VALUE-ANALYSIS

<u>Instructions</u>:

Have the class do a value-analysis of a paragraph from literature. The selection should be one that attempts to define or explain the meaning of one of the value areas. The sample given below is taken from the Phillips translation of the New Testament: The key thoughts have been underlined for comparison with other "definitions" or illustrations (i.e. from the movies or TV) of the concept of affection.

I Corinthians 13:4-8

"This love of which I speak is <u>slow to lose patience</u>--it <u>looks for a way of being constructive</u>. It is <u>not possessive</u>: it is <u>neither anxious to impress</u> nor does it cherish inflated ideas of its own importance.

Love <u>has good manners</u> and <u>does not pursue selfish advantage</u>. It <u>is not touchy</u>. It <u>does not keep account of evil</u> or gloat over the wickedness of other people. On the contrary, <u>it is glad with all good men when truth prevails</u>.

Love <u>knows not limit to its endurance</u>, <u>no end to its trust</u>, <u>no fading of its hope</u>; it <u>can outlast anything</u>. It is, in fact, <u>the one thing that still stands when all else has fallen</u>."

MY FRIENDS

Instructions:

    List the names of as many friends as possible under each category.

Friends that are girls:

Friends that are boys:

Friends that are grown-ups:

Friends that are animals:

13

RESPECT

Activities Related to Understanding
The Respect Value Area

DEFINITION: *Courtesy and admiration that you have for other people and they have for you. Having someone that you look up to.*

DESCRIPTIVE BEHAVIORS: *Those behaviors that affect the way you employ your individual talents to achieve a recognized social role and self-esteem for yourself and others.*

BEHAVIORAL OBJECTIVES (Principal Value Goals): *Self-identity, a recognized social role, and self-esteem without fear of undeserved deprivation or penalties from others.*

The following activities are designed to increase the student's understanding of the *respect* value area. Where feasible, an activity should include not only some discussion of the activity, but also, more importantly, its application to the student's own life. While the activities presented range from early elementary through adult level, most can be adapted to suit the age or comprehension of a particular group of students.

1. Discuss the idea that respect is usually earned through performance. Thus, anything you do well may earn respect from your peers.

2. Choose a secret friend in the classroom and write one or two lines telling why you respect that person.

3. Ma, e a chart showing some of the ways a child might earn respect in the classroom. Refer to it occasionally.

4. Have children mark a continuum as to how highly they feel people respect them in various areas.

5. Discuss what might happen if:
   a. We did not respect the laws of the country.
   b. We did not respect the school rules.
   c. We did not respect the class rules.

6. Have a child's desk in the middle of the room. That child is "Child of Day". He may be first in everything that day — first to pass out balls, papers, etc. Have the desk change "magically" in the night.

7. Read "Who's Polite" to the Class.

8. "Who am I?" bulletin board. Use baby pictures and child-made clues.

9. Write a story about "What I wish I were like." Illustrate.

10. Have the class list activities which will help create a positive self-image.

11. Analyze newspaper articles.

12. Show film and discuss the interaction of people.

13. Keep a diary.

14. Daily self-evaluation (How I feel about myself).

15. Make a collage of faces showing different moods.

16. Make a "my best work box" with individual folders for children to place work they are proud of. Visitors should be encouraged to examine the work and papers sent home periodically.

17. Clarify difference between right and privilege.

18. Have a "Meet So-and-So" activity: each child introduces and tells class about another child in the class, stressing his good traits.

19. Give out awards at the end of the year (month?) for each child. (Friendliest, Best Helper, etc.)

20. Have a discussion about borrowing: a. with permission, b. handle carefully, c. return promptly.

21. Show a movie about the flag. Discuss such questions as, why do you think we have a flag? Did the flag always look the way it does today? How should we handle the flag? What does the flag represent?

22. Draw pictures illustrating ways a person might show respect to his country.

23. Plan a flag ceremony and invite another class or classes to attend.

**The following are some examples
of worksheets for students.**

RESPECT IN ACTION

A. Draw a picture of what you are doing to show respect for others:

B. Draw a picture of what you are doing to notice respect given to you:

C. Draw a picture of what someone else is doing to show respect to you:

RESPECT ON TV

Instructions:

Have the class review a TV guide or other such sources for information on the TV programs they watch. Develop a list of enhancement and deprivation type programs for each value area. The sample given below is for Respect, but the same format can be used for affection, skill, etc. Remember, we are looking for the children's perceptions of programs offered on TV. Since TV is a major source for learning, modeling, and image-development, the children should be encouraged to analyze the amount of enhancing or depriving TV they watch, and possibly, make some personal commitments regarding watching habits.

Some possible examples:

ENHANCING	DEPRIVATIONAL
Partridge Family	All in the Family
Room 222	Sanford and Son
Mr. Rogers	Laugh-In
Electric Company	Odd Couple
Captain Kangeroo	Love American Style
Wide World of Sports	I Love Lucy
This is Your Life	Don Rickles
Walt Disney	Paul Lynde
Walton Family	Maude
What's My Line	Cartoons
Romper Room	Soap Operas
City Kids	
Zoom	

14

SKILL

Activities Related to Understanding
The Skill Value Area

DEFINITION: *The ability to do things well and to feel that you can do them well.*

DESCRIPTIVE BEHAVIORS: *Those behaviors that affect the development of our own and others' talents and abilities within the limits of our resources and potentials.*

BEHAVIORAL OBJECTIVES (Principal Value Goals): *Provide opportunities for each student to develop his talents to the limits of his potential.*

The following activities are designed to increase the student's understanding of the *skill* value area. Where feasible, an activity should include not only some discussion of the activity, but also, more importantly, its application to the student's own life. While the activities presented range from early elementary through adult level, most can be adapted to suit the age or comprehension of a particular group of students.

1. List on the blackboard skills needed to get one through an ordinary day. Begin with getting up in the morning and end up at bedtime.

2. Discuss giving-up. Why do people give up? How do they feel when they decide to give-up? When should you give-up, and when should you keep trying?

3. Read the story in the Primer reading textbook, "Janet and the New Skates". What skill did she lack? How did it make her feel? Was Mark skillful in skating? How did it make him feel?

4. Choose a story from the State-adopted Basal readers which points out an area of enhancement or deprivation of skill and the resulting feelings of the characters involved.

5. Read story about famous athlete.

6. Visit a bakery, garage, etc. — evaluate the skills used (trade skills).   •

7. Make a list of basic skills all people need by kindergarten — can be extended to any time span.

8. Have child make a comparative list. Head one column "Skills I Have". Head the other column "Skills I'd Like to Learn". Can be used for discussion or other suitable activity.

9. Certificates can be given out to a child who shows a marked improvement in a skill. (They don't have to be best — just improved.)

10. Study some historical or present-day figures that became famous because of a special skill they had.

11. Have the children pretend they wanted to become a good base-ball catcher but they had never played real baseball before. Have them identify what they would have to do and learn to try and accomplish this goal. List all ideas on oak tag strips, then arrange them according to what they would have to do first, second, etc. Do this activity with several other new skills and see if a pattern develops in the what to do and learn portion.

12. Discuss in what ways size, age, physical and mental abilities affect what skills a person might possess.

13. Make a chart. Teacher writes the simple definition of skill. The children all make a small picture of a skill of their choice and paste the pictures below the definition. Refer to it when the opportunity arises.

14. Discuss the skills a two or three year old possesses. List the skills the children have that the young child does not have.

15. Make a skill list — watch it grow over the year's time.

16. Children cut pictures from magazines which demonstrate a variety of skills. Paste on large oak tag. Allow each child to point out those things he can do.

**The following are some examples
of worksheets for students.**

CONCEPT WHEEL

On a large bulletin board create a "wagon wheel" approximately 6 feet in diameter with several spokes and a "hub" about 12 inches in diameter.

In the center of the wheel, place a card containing a value word previously discussed by the group.

Children bring items or pictures, etc. to illustrate concepts, and they place them in the wheel. Repeat for each value area.

BECOMING AWARE OF VALUES

CREATIVE WRITING

Dial-A-Story

CHARACTER (list on a wheel):
ladybug, old woman, inventor, ghost, soldier,
prince, dwarf, scientist, cannibal, children,
giant, monster, teacher, little boy, witch,
spaceman, robot, policeman, mother, king,
fairy, puppy, step-mother, horse ...

TRAIT
clever, idiot, famous, ragged, greedy, wicked
faithful, lonely, terrible, beautiful, grate-
ful, strange, naughty, miserable, rude,
grumbling, astonished, bad-tempered, jealous,
dumb, clumsy, foolish, scared, successful ...

LOCATION

Africa, prison, garden, space station, desert
restaurant, mountain, castle, island, deep in
the forest, Mars, under the bed, in a cave,
on top of the table, on a train, at the zoo,
in an airplane, Switzerland, in a tent,
submarine, underground, dungeon, moon, scout
room ...

CIRCUMSTANCES
lived all alone, shipwrecked, frightened, had
to do all the work, beasts were fleeing, had
no friends, smeared with ink, did not know
answers, scolded for being late, no way to
leave, banished, brakes fail, alarm didn't
go off, had a flat tire, had to walk a mile,
afraid to go home, found a treasure, light
went out, saw strange footprints, wild
animals passed close by, swallowed by a whale
defeated, invaded by ..., day-dreaming ...

BASIC NEEDS
affection, respect, skill, enlightenment,
influence, wealth, well-being, responsibilit

LIST OF SKILLS

NAME _____

    Below is a list of the members of your class.
Today's assignment is to write something that you
think each person <u>can do well</u>. The purpose of thi
is to get you to find good things in your class-
mates. It illustrates the value of skill.

NAME
(Members of class)

<u>SOMETHING HE OR SHE CAN DO
WELL</u>

15

ENLIGHTENMENT

Activities Related to Understanding The Enlightenment Value Area

DEFINITION: *Your ability to understand what things mean, and using your knowledge to help you do the things you want to do.*

DESCRIPTIVE BEHAVIORS: *Those behaviors that affect the way we seek understanding about ourselves and the world we live in; which includes education and the interpretation of personal experience.*

BEHAVIORAL OBJECTIVES (Principal Value Goals): *Provide experiences for awareness and openness, and encourage students to find their own truth in every issue without losing sight of social norms and the significant events of human achievement.*

The following activities are designed to increase the student's understanding of the *enlightenment* value area. Where feasible, an activity should include not only some discussion of the activity, but also, more importantly, its application to the student's own life. While the activities presented range from early elementary through adult level, most can be adapted to suit the age or comprehension of a particular group of students.

1. Compare and contrast countries' wealth to numbers of educated people.

2. Find out how many homes in the classroom subscribe to a daily newspaper. Question parents as to what are the favorite parts of the paper. Report findings.

3. Children set their own standards wherever possible; i.e., how many words they think they can learn for the next week, etc.

4. Invite someone in who is going to college. Have children question the person to find out why he is going. What he is learning that he couldn't learn at home? How does he expect to benefit from this enlightenment?

5. Have children write down the names of the magazines their parents subscribe to. Graph the responses.

6. List twenty words on the board. Circle the words that the majority of the children would not have understood last year. Erase the one or two difficult words that they may not understand for several more years. Invite a couple of sixth graders in to see if they understand *all* the words.

7. Discuss: Could a child take an adult's job? Could a girl age six do everything her mother does in the home as well?

8. Analyze a T.V. program.

9. When a child has done some outside learning, or just seems to know a little extra about something, he can be declared the "Expert Authority on XXX".

10. Children test each other — Everyone thinks of a question about something you have been studying and asks another person in the class, one by one, so the others can hear the question and answer.

11. Teacher outlines on the blackboard new learnings acquired so far this year in math, etc.

12. Define enlightenment using the simplified value definition.

13. Use the word in sentences designed to tell what kind of things they already know.

14. Cut pictures from a catalog, magazine, etc. of objects which might contribute to enlightenment of an individual. Such as radio, books, telescope, etc. Paste them on a large sheet of paper titled, *Things Which Help Us Learn.*

15. Have resource people come to the class.

16. Act out "What if there were no school". Evaluate.

17. Take frequent photographs of children engaged in individual projects in the classroom. Display and send home.

18. Blindfold walk: Discuss "trusting". Blindfold a child (or yourself) and have another child guide him. Discuss how a blind person feels.

19. Write down a list of inventions we need by the year 2000.

20. Make up a game and play it with a friend.

21. Plan a space trip. We can never come back. What three things would we take?

22. Create as many flowers as you can that are not now existing.

23. Describe how it would feel to be a color, or month. (e.g. Sept., yellow, fall leaf, Oct., orange, pumpkin etc).

24. Give a child a word to act out.

25. What would you see if you were looking down on earth from a space ship?

26. Describe yourself using letters in your name (e.g. Angel Nice Nimble; use nouns, verbs or adjectives etc.).

27. Discuss the affects of labeling; role-play a situation where someone has been labeled "a good athlete, a good student, a poor sport, etc.).

28. Write a five-line story using five unrelated words (e.g. snowflake, scissors, ocean etc.).

29. Each child writes a beginning to a story. Trade papers and have another child finish it.

30. Have the child stretch out on butcher paper. Outline his body and have him cut it out. The child then cuts out pictures of what he likes to do and pastes it on his figure. It becomes "me".

31. Have children create problems for each other to solve.

32. Write animal cinquains; guess what child is describing.

33. Read "Jack and the Beanstalk" story. Rewrite it: What if Jack was Jackie — a girl?

34. Write a story using pictures.

35. Write alliteration sentences. Act out.

36. Role playing. For example, act out receiving a poor report card.

37. Have two children come into the class arguing. Stop the argument. Send three others out of the room, and have one at a time come back and report his interpretation. Compare, contrast the various observations.

38. Have the class observe the appearance of a child. The child then leaves and changes his appearance. Upon returning, discuss this change. How can appearance change your life?

39. As the teacher, give directions that cause confusion eg. tell the class to sit anywhere they want, write on paper etc. Then discuss freedom without rules; what happens?

40. Discuss environmental changes, how would they affect behavior? e.g. no desks, no students, etc.?

41. Discuss or write guessing games.
    1. Which is sneakier; mud or midnight?
    2. Which is quicker; yellow or black?
    3. Which is louder; a smile or a frown?

26. Write paradoxes; I am so happy I could cry, etc.

27. Design a school. What would you teach? What supplies would you buy? What would it look like?

44. Each child is given $100.00. If he were rich, what would he buy? If he were poor, what would he buy? Compare these lists.

45. Each child is on a desert island with only animals and birds. How would he communicate?

46. If only five books could be left in the world, what should they be?

**The following are some examples
of worksheets for students.**

HOW TO LEARN

Describe ways a person can go about learning something he (she) wants to know.

1.

2.

3.

4.

5.

6.

7.

8.

9.

10.

LOOKING AND LISTENING

List reasons for people reading, watching TV,
writing, listening.

1.

2.

3.

4.

5.

6.

7.

8.

9.

10.

THE NEW PET

Instructions:

Have children pretend they found a strange little lizard (or bird, or other animals suitable to your area) who seemed to be injured. They wished to care for it and make it their pet.

What would they need to know?

Where might they seek enlightenment on this subject?

16

INFLUENCE

Activities Related to Understanding
The Influence Value Area

DEFINITION: *To control your own behavior and make other people see your point-of-view and do what you would like them to do. Being able to make your own choices based on good information. (Note: Some use the word "Power" instead of "Influence.")*

DESCRIPTIVE BEHAVIORS: *Those behaviors which affect the way we participate as individuals and with others in the decision-making process of living together in home, job, community, and beyond; including the exertion of personal influence and power.*

BEHAVIORAL OBJECTIVES (Principal Value Goals): *Participation in making important decisions and exerting informal influence according to one's talents and responsibilities.*

The following activities are designed to increase the student's understanding of the *influence* value area. Where feasible, an activity should include not only some discussion of the activity, but also, more importantly, its application to the student's own life. While the activities presented range from early elementary through adult level, most can be adapted to suit the age or comprehension of a particular group of students.

1. Role play:
   a. One child asks another to go home to play after school. Respondent declines offer.
   b. First child offers her candy bar from her lunch if she will go. Child agrees to the arrangement.

2. Occasionally have a ten minute period where a child will exchange places with the teacher.

3. Elect a room library committee. Have them set up the library, formulate operating procedures, library rules, etc.

4. Teacher reads many stories in which the character or characters must make some obvious decisions. Have children identify what the decisions were, what might have been the alternatives, etc.

5. John is walking home with a group of friends. Two people want him to go to their house to play. What will he decide to do? How will he go about deciding?

6. Discuss the idea that decisions are choices made from alternatives and they have consequences.

7. Have children work with a hypothetical situation. They must decide whether to go to the beach, the park, or the bowling alley. Write or tell the probable consequences of their decision.

8. Children think of some decision they have made recently and share with the class the steps they followed in making that decision.

9. Have children make a picture of what they would like to be when they grow up. Children should then research to find out schooling required, duties of the job, etc. Make a bulletin board out of the materials titled: Citizens of 1986, etc.

10. Let children develop a list of questions they want to ask their parents about making choices and why. Discuss.

11. Read biographies of famous people and discuss decisions that enabled them to become famous.

12. Study the life of a President. Examine how some decisions made during his Presidency have influenced our lives today.

13. Cut from local paper articles telling some recent decisions made by the city council. Discuss in what way those decisions will affect them personally or their families.

14. Illustrate decisions your parents make for you. Such as what to eat, time for bed, etc.

15. Discuss the decisions the teacher makes for you.

16. Give children a number of situations in which they must choose:
    a. You are very hot. Which choice will you make? Going for a swim or eating an ice cream cone? Why?
    b. It's your day to choose what game will be played during gym. What game will you choose and why?

17. List all decisions made since sunrise or in last 24 hours, then rank in order of importance.

18. Show film strip and discuss the importance of thinking for one's self.

20. Elicit all simple decisions made by children.

21. Each child to list ways he uses his influence. How he is enhanced and how he is deprived.

22. Ask each child to write down or tell one important decision they have made in their lives. Ask them to write down what decision they think will be the most important one in their whole lives. Post results.

23. Read a story from the Value Readers (*Human Value Series* — Arnspiger, Rucker & Brill). Stop, however, at the point where a decision needs to be made. As a creative writing activity, have the children list two different alternatives the main character could choose from, and the possible consequences of each.

24. Early in the year before the children have read it for themselves, read the story "Eat It and Have It" in *Around the Corner*. Stop before Mr. Green suggests taking a picture of the fish, and discuss Mark's problem, and children can suggest alternative solutions.

181

25. Have a language arts lesson — "Crazy Ideas" where a situation is suggested, like "a person buys too many groceries to carry home. What can he do?" The children suggest three crazy solutions (alternatives) like "kick the groceries home; strap the eggs on the dog's back, etc."; then when these are on the board, children tell what consequences would result from each of these solutions.

26. At the end of each day (for one week), each child writes down the most important thing that happened that day. At the end of the week, have each circle the most important thing that happened all week. Discuss with child if you think alternate thing may have been involved.

27. Value-analyze classroom situations and predict possible problems and solutions.

28. Have the class discuss some of the following topics. Have them decide which were wise decisions and which were not and WHY.
    a. How they spend their free time.
    b. What TV shows to see.
    c. What games they'll play and with whom.
    d. What friends they will choose.

29. Quickie decision — teacher-made problems. Time limit for solution. Share finding and evaluate.

30. Elect a chairman to serve on a weekly or monthly basis. The chairman can lead opening ceremonies by calling on other people to check attendance, flag, windows, sharing calendar, etc. Evaluate the chairman and define the qualities of an effective chairman.

31. Look for reasons for antisocial actions.

32. Children can cite examples of times when decisions are made FOR a group (what kind of decisions, and who makes them, and why) and times when decisions are made BY a group (what kind of decisions, how they arrive at the decision, and why).

33. Visit a City Council meeting and discuss use of influence in society.

34. Write one thing you have done today to help someone. Write one thing you did today that deprived someone else of something. Do not sign name. Class evaluates in terms of value categories.

35. Invite principal to discuss power of his office. Enhancements and deprivations. Have him discuss some of the important decisions he must make for the school.

36. Research role of press in influencing use of power. (voting, pressure groups, etc.)

37. Read story in Value Readers on power. Discuss enhancements and deprivation.

38. Make a scrapbook of articles relating to influence decision-making.

39. Discuss risks involved in everyday activities, such as walking to school, etc.

40. Children name several things they consider a "risk". Decide which of these are big risks, and which are little risks.

41. Use examples from the news, like the space shots, etc., and define the degree of risk involved and the gain.

42. Give the children a set of circumstances they may find themselves in, which will require a decision. The children must decide if their decision is one of high-risk/high-gain, low-risk/high-gain, or what the combination of risk to gain is. For example: "Some one dares you to hang by your feet from the monkey bars; and you are considering whether to do it or not."

43. Make a classroom scrapbook of articles relating to decision-making (influence). Investigate reasons for decisions.

44. Read a story from the Value Readers which illustrates power. Discuss or role-play the ending.

45. Have a small group of children preview a film and have them vote to decide whether it should be shown to the class.

46. Make a picture booklet on influence. Illustrate one time you persuaded someone to do something for you. Illustrate one time you voted for something important. Illustrate something you had to do because it was the law. Illustrate some group situation in which you had total influence.

47. Act out the fable "The Sun and the Wind". Discuss the influence of both as used in the story.

48. President and class monitors elected instead of appointed; Children vote on how they liked a film, assembly, etc.; Children pick up and hand in work themselves instead of having it passed

out and collected; Children decide for themselves what they will do when their work is finished — clay, library books, or whatever; Discuss the people they think are very important, and what important people or leaders do.

49. Formulate possible methods of equalizing influence (Sharing of influence).

50. Discuss role of authority figures (principal, teacher) in influence structure.

**The following are some examples
of worksheets for students.**

ALTERNATIVES

Instructions:

A. Have children state, explain, and expand upon a problem in their own words.

B. Make a long list of alternatives without any discussion of the "goodness" of any suggestions.

C. Select a number (say 10) of the "best" alternatives as determined by the group.

D. Pick the "best of the best" and value-analyze for its enhancing effects on all involved.

PROBLEM-SOLVING

(Situations for young children)

1. Someone is teasing you.
2. Front door is locked and no one is home.
3. Bike has a flat tire.
4. I went outside and the dog got away.
5. I don't like my mommy to get mad at me.
6. I skinned my knee.
7. I'm hungry and Mom is busy.
8. I can't find anything to wear to bed.
9. I can't find any friends to play with.
10. I broke a glass.
11. It's raining and I'm in the house with nothing to do.
12. A neighbor boy took my toy away from me.
13. My older sister doesn't want to watch the TV program I want to watch.
14. My brother and I both want the toy out of the cereal box.

DECISIONS TODAY

Today I made these decisions <u>myself</u>!

Today other people made these decisions for me.

17

WEALTH

Activities Related to Understanding
The Wealth Value Area

DEFINITION: *The goods and services people need and want in their everyday lives.*

DESCRIPTIVE BEHAVIORS: *Those behaviors which affect the facilities, products and services we provide for the welfare and wealth of ourselves and others.*

BEHAVIORAL OBJECTIVES (Principal Value Goals): *Active interest and involvement in producing goods and services for others and oneself.*

The following activities are designed to increase the student's understanding of the *wealth* value area. Where feasible, an activity should include not only some discussion of the activity, but also, more importantly, its application to the student's own life. While the activities presented range from early elementary through adult level, most can be adapted to suit the age or comprehension of a particular group of students.

1. Discuss now possessing things doesn't necessarily lead to happiness.

2. Discuss the idea that, for many people, a willingness to work hard will increase their wealth. Draw a picture of something they would be willing to do if they would be paid 25¢.

3. Discuss relationship of skill and enlightenment to wealth.

4. Read and discuss stories designed to further understand wealth.

5. Research to find out how some extremely rich people made their fortunes.

6. Problem solving for role playing: A child wants a toy, but it costs quite a bit of money. What can he do?

7. Read "My Dime" to the class. Discuss story. Why did both children want the dime? How did they use the money? (Reader: Primer Level *Around the Corner* Harper & Row).

8. List some reasons a person might *need* to buy a bicycle. List reasons a person may *want* to buy a bicycle.

9. Divide a large paper into four sections. Have children illustrate services which are performed for them.

10. Have children pretend they are on a life raft alone with no hope of being saved for several days. What *things* would they most want for these next few days.

11. List community services performed for us which one could class as essential. List one or two which could be classified non-essential.

12. Have each child draw pictures or make a list of all the goods (wealth) they personally own.

13. Using the interview technique, go through a day in the life of a child in your classroom. Call attention to services which are performed for the child. Example: Who made your breakfast, washed your clothes; the crossing guard, street cleaner, school secretary, school lunch workers, etc.

14. Research and discuss various forms of wealth in different cultures.

15. Cut pictures from magazines which illustrate various forms of wealth.

The following are some examples of worksheets for students.

WEALTH WORDS

Can you think of "wealth words" that start with
each of the letters in WEALTH?

W   is for _____

E   is for _____

A   is for _____

L   is for _____

T   is for _____

H   is for _____

PIONEER DAYS

List some things that would be considered "wealth" to a boy or girl growing up in the pioneer days of America:

GOODS
(things they have)

SERVICES
(things they could do for others)

WEALTH FOR ME

List some things that make you wealthy:

GOODS
(things you have)

SERVICES
(things you can do for others)

18

WELL-BEING

Activities Related to Understanding
The Well-Being Value Area

DEFINITION: *An inner feeling of contentment, health, inner-peace and happiness. Not being sick, worried, upset or unhappy.*

DESCRIPTIVE BEHAVIORS: *Those behaviors which affect the development and care of our human resources including the physical and mental health of ourselves and others.*

BEHAVIORAL OBJECTIVES (Principal Value Goals):*Improvement in mental and physical health.*

The following activities are designed to increase the student's understanding of the *well-being* value area. Where feasible, an activity should include not only some discussion of the activity, but also, more importantly, its application to the student's own life. While the activities presented range from early elementary through adult level, most can be adapted to suit the age or comprehension of a particular group of students.

1. Talk about medical emergencies: what to do, who to call, where to go.

2. Ask nurse what happens at school when illness or injury occurs.

3. Talk about what to do when we feel bad — find something else to do, talk it out, play a game, etc.

4. Look at pictures of people and describe how each one feels.

5. Do sentence completions such as:
   Losing the game made me ....
   My neighbor is ....
   When I lied I ....
   The first day of school I ....

6. Write or verbally do story completions.

7. Write "Happiness Is" books.

8. A sense of well-being and fun can be promoted through music and songs.

9. Draw "Happy Day", "Sad Day", "My Best Day", etc. pictures. Collect and make class books to be shared by all.

10. List the characteristics we like in friends.

11. Talk about how we can make new friends.

12. What should we do when we quarrel?

13. Define good health.

14. Have lessons about good breakfasts, hours of sleep, etc.

15. Play soft music to calm class after recess.

16. Four basic food groups — have the children come up and place pictures in the right category on the bulletin board.

17. The children may wish to find out what children in other lands eat for breakfast, lunch and dinner. Compare their menus with "ours". Discuss why their habits are different from ours.

18. Keep a record of your meals. Discuss nutrition in daily school lunches.

19. Have children choose P.E. activities for a week, stressing the need to develop different skills and exercise various parts of the body.

20. Define well-being as physical and mental.

21. Invite doctor (nurse) to make presentation concerning relationship between physical and mental health.

22. Make a list of "feeling words." List them on the chalk board.

23. Let the children tell about times when they were sad, happy, angry, afraid and worried.

24. List things that modify moods and feelings.

25. Discuss happenings at school which make us feel bad.

26. Make a mural of a happy day or week. Activities and episodes which enhance children's well-being.

27. Have children draw a happy face on one side of the paper and a sad face on the back. As you name situations, they may hold up the face showing their reaction, i.e., going to school, being sick, telling a lie, losing their lunch money, being pushed in line, pushing in line, etc.

28. Explain that well-being means feeling well and being happy.

29. Collect scrapbooks of healthy people.

30. Discuss growth. Measure each child in the room. Record with child's name on a long strip attached to wall. Mark strip *Watch Us Grow.* Repeat this activity often.

**The following are some examples
of worksheets for students.**

HAPPINESS FOLDERS

Instructions:

1. Have each child make his own happiness folde
2. Each day have him draw a picture of somethin
   that makes him happy and explain to the righ
   of the picture why it makes him happy.
3. Value-analyze folders for emphasis or lack o
   emphasis in each value area.
4. Use analysis for strategy planning.

HOME SAFETY

THINGS TO DO

1. Have children conduct a safety check in the home with their parents to see that items are stored properly.

2. Make or purchase labels that children could paste on dangerous products found in the home.

3. Dramatize situations where people have mistaken dangerous products for some other non-harmful substance.

FEELING GOOD

Make a list of at least three things you feel are important to your well-being:

PHYSICAL WELL-BEING

1.

2.

3.

4.

5.

MENTAL WELL-BEING

1.

2.

3.

4.

5.

WELL-BEING ACROSTIC

List nine words that show "well-being", each one beginning with one of well-being's letters.

W   is for _____

E   is for _____

L   is for _____

L   is for _____

B   is for _____

E   is for _____

I   is for _____

N   is for _____

G   is for _____

HAPPY PEOPLE

WHAT WOULD MAKE YOU MORE HAPPY?

WHAT WOULD MAKE YOU MORE HEALTHY?

THIS IS A LIST OF THINGS I CAN DO TO HELP OTHERS
BE HAPPY OR HEALTHY:

19

RESPONSIBILITY

Activities Related to Understanding
The Responsibility Value Area

DEFINITION: *Knowing what is right and wrong for oneself. Keeping one's promises and being honest and just and trustworthy. (Note some use the word "Rectitude" instead of "Responsibility.")*

DESCRIPTIVE BEHAVIORS: *Those behaviors which affect the moral responsibility we assume toward ourselves and others, including standards for our own behavior.*

BEHAVIORAL OBJECTIVES (Principal Value Goals): *To develop a sense of responsibility for one's own behavior, consideration for others, and a high sense of integrity.*

The following activities are designed to increase the student's understanding of the responsibility value area. Where feasible, an activity should include not only some discussion of the activity, but also, more importantly, its application to the student's own life. While the activities presented range from early elementary through adult level, most can be adapted to suit the age or comprehension of a particular group of students.

1. Show filmstrips with recorded, open-ended stories.

2. Have children sign up to help other people in various skills such as reading, math, spelling, etc.

3. Discuss responsibility for one's own behavior — doing the right thing, sharing values.

4. Have a classroom discussion about telling the truth, making promises, etc. Role-play various problems that come up in the classroom, and think of different ways the problems could be solved. Discuss courtesy. Practice courteous acts — a pretend visitor with introductions, etc.

5. Ask children to illustrate a playground situation that shows fair play. Have children record their feelings about their behavior on a prepared ditto (happy-sad faces) and then put it away. Take it out again in two weeks or a month, and compare how they feel now with how they felt then. No one sees it but the child.

6. Formulate rules of behavior for a field trip. Discuss why they are necessary.

7. Discuss situation where we obey authority. Analyze "why" of alternatives to a situation. What should you do if you find money? Set up class standards and discuss why we need class rules. What is expected lunchroom behavior and why is it necessary?

8. Take a walking field trip to observe some rules which are observed by the people who live in the community. Example: traffic and pedestrian rules, litter laws, etc. Look for examples of violations of community rules — what happened?

9. During one recess, have class observe playground rules being observed. List what rules were followed, which were not and what happened as a result.

10. Discuss the difference between playground rules (safety oriented) and classroom rules (mostly orderly rules).

11. Dramatize trying to learn and study when no one observed the rules of order.

12. Discuss rules followed at home. Tell how the rules help them.

13. Discuss crimes mentioned in newspaper.

14. Discuss taking things from a store.

15. Why do people take other people's bicycles? What are solutions to this common problem?

16. Talk about "treating others the way you would like to be treated."

17. List some examples of unfair practices in the classroom and on the playground — not sharing ball, etc.

18. Discuss why it is important to keep a promise. How do we feel if someone breaks a promise?

19. What rules do we follow in institutions other than school?

20. Why do we have traffic rules, and what would happen if we didn't follow them?

21. Formulate a list of rules showing how one nation should treat another nation.

22. Have children think about a rule they have for themselves which is not an enforced rule. Draw a picture of their rule. Ask, "Where did you first get the idea for your rule?"

23. Discuss the concept "honor".

**The following are some examples
of worksheets for students.**

PERSONAL ACTIVITIES SCHEDULE

Instructions:

Each child can develop his own personal responsibility chart which can be in the home or at school. Each day the child can award himself (a star or some other symbol) for completion of his personal responsibilities. The sample shown below includes: a) brushing teeth morning and night, b) eating something from each of the basic food groups, c) doing assigned homework, d) getting to bed on time and resting the necessary number of hours, e) completing assigned duties at home or school, f) having some recreation or exercise time, and g) taking a bath or shower as scheduled.

Activity	Mon	Tue	Wed	Thu	Fri	Sat	Sun

WHAT WOULD YOU DO?

(Picture of messy yard.)	Answer
(Picture of finding a lost wallet.)	Answer
(Picture of dropping and breaking a glass on the floor.)	Answer

SECTION THREE

VARIOUS HELPFUL DATA

20

FOR PRINCIPALS ONLY

We have included two items which should be of particular interest to principals. The first, an assignment to be given to students in a classroom setting, produces some interesting insights into the role of the principal, as evidenced by the quotations.

The second item was actually prepared by the principal and office staff of an elementary school which has incorporated the valuing approach. The suggestions are the result of direct experience and should be very helpful in setting up a valuing program.

INSTRUCTIONS

Have your class write a word, phrase, or paragraph on each of the rules followed or duties done by the principal (as seen by them). Send the results to the principal for his own enlightenment. Ask him to note both the bad and good points and suggest ways (if possible) to strengthen his image in the eyes of the children

The following are direct quotes from student responses to their assignment:

"He goes around and makes announcements. He works almost all day. At lunch time he eats lunch. When we are noisy in the cafeteria he quiets us down. At recess, when we go out to play, he talks with the teachers. Before school opens he has coffee with the teachers."

"He gos s to classrooms and makes announcements. If Mary is busy, then I show notes to him. When it is raining in the lunch room he tells us to wait."

"The principal goes in classrooms. He shows films after school in the lunch room. They are good too! He talks to teachers. Sometimes he goes out on the playground."

"A principal takes care of the school. He helps Boy Scouts or Cub Scouts, B.S.A. He helps with plays and goes to classrooms to give us announcements. He works in woodshop with bigger boys. Sometimes he is a substitute."

"He makes lots of reports and has meetings with other teachers. He tells us lots of things. He makes many announcements and makes carnivals too."

"A principal makes up rules. He comes to your room to tell you about stuff. He also has a desk. The principal is very nice to the kids. I think he stays to 5 o'clock. Do you?"

"He comes out when the fire bell rings. He tells the kids to get off the wet grass on to the playground."

"A principal makes some of the rules. The principal helps boys get out of fights. The principal makes announcements to rooms. He takes care of the school. He's the teacher's boss. He makes rules for the playground. Principals have to get a Doctor's Degree first to be a principal for a school. He fixes up the place where we eat. One time when I was in second grade, he let us use his colored t.v. It was his t.v. from home. We had it in our room for a long time. This principal is the only one I've had."

"A principal does lots of things. He makes announcements. Sometimes he comes and teaches."

"A principal tells announcements. He works in his office and does things. He goes on the playground and watches us. Then, he goes back to his office and does more things. He talks to us when we are bad or sometimes good. I like our principal. Principals are not mean, the children make them mad."

"He goes around making announcements. If some boy or girl breaks the rules they will be sent to the principal."

"He makes announcements and does work. He tells us about things and he helps us remember things. He comes in the lunch room when it rains. He finds lunches."

"He works a lot! He makes announcements all over the school. He gives us rules, some that I don't know. But I think they are always good. He is very nice too! When I go in the office I look in his room. There he is in his room working all the time! Sometimes he is on our playground watching everybody play."

"I don't know but I think he does a lot of announcements. He passes notes out at the gate."

"A principal does paper work. He teaches for a teacher who has an appointment somewhere."

"A principal goes to the classes and talks to the boys and girls. Some of the time he tells the teachers what to do. Sometimes he goes to the lunch room and tells the children what to do when it rains."

"He goes around making announcements. Spanks bad children. Talks to fathers and mothers. Takes childrens temperatures."

"A principal makes announcements and rules. No gum in the school. You cannot run on the blacktop, because you can fall and cut your knee. No spitting or you will get in trouble."

"He hands out awards. He asks the teachers where they want to go on their field trips. He talks to the secretary. Sometimes he goes out on lunch recess and talks to you. He is also very, very nice. He says "Hi" to you."

"He goes around and tells the people if there is going to be a carnival or whatever is going to happen. When people think they are sick, he tells them if they can go home to rest. On rainy days he tells people when they can go to their classrooms. If the rain stops he tells them if they can go outside and play. He tells them not to step in any puddles."

"He makes announcements. He makes sure that no one fights at recess and makes sure that no one gets hurt."

"He makes announcements in the class rooms. He talks to kids if they are fighting."

"He takes care of the school. He scolds boys and girls when they're bad. When it is raining he helps in the cafeteria. Sometimes he puts up the tether balls."

"He helps us when we need it. He helps Willard too. And he plays tether ball."

"A principal takes care of the school yard. He helps boys and girls that get hurt. He comes to give papers to Mrs. Walters. He takes care of the school. He helps with the film when it doesn't work."

"The principal makes the rules. He takes care of the school."

"He tells us when there are movies. He stops the fights. He gives orders."

"The principal makes announcements. He works in the office. He talks to the teachers about things. Sometimes he takes out the tether balls."

CONCEPT: A PRINCIPAL'S ROLE

Here are some suggestions for use in the Values Approach prepared by the principal and office staff of an elementary school.

1. Principal should use the "modeling" approach (show affection, respect, etc. to children and teachers).

2. Principal should write "sunshine" notes to teachers after observations.

3. Principal should encourage children to come to office to show him their creative work and arrange with teachers to make this possible.

4. When principal observes good things children are doing, he should stop to tell them about it, or write a note to the child, thereby encouraging his staff to do the same.

5. The Values Approach can be used as the subjects for Creative Art on Office Bulletin Boards, or in the Nurses' Office. They can be changed often, bringing attention to different situations and value areas.

6. The Media Center can make a Value Manual which suggests suitable books and A V materials. Bulletin boards can also be used to either "tell a story" in art or to depict a book which fits a valuing area.

7. The Principal should involve the teachers in decision-making that affects the entire school program both in curriculum, and budget planning.

8. The Student Council is a good way to help the children make decisions — also they can come up with ideas that show value sharing. A Newsletter, for example, might be published and distributed which would be popular and stimulate children's thinking and decision-making for low-risk/high-gain behavior.

9. The role of the Support Teacher should be lessened in the discipline area and enlarged in the area of Values Approach — involving the children who are most unsure of themselves and who need encouragement the most.

10. The minority group children should be encouraged in the Values Approach by letting them see models of older children and students who have succeeded that they can identify with. Also this would encourage other children of the majority group to appreciate the good things in the minority culture pattern and therefore build up the minority child's self-image. (Cross-age teaching is a good pattern for this.)

11. The secretary can incorporate the Values Approach in many areas — one of these is to show concern and love when a child comes into the office because of injury or sickness.

12. When emergency first aid is applied, she should follow up with the parent to show the school's concern and therefore help to make a closer bond between the home and school.

13. When a child comes into the office, he should receive the same courteous treatment as if he were an adult. This doesn't mean that he should be allowed to "overrun" the school, but it does mean that he should be listened to and helped to make a good choice about his being in the office. He should find it a pleasant, helpful place when needed, not a place that is feared.

14. The Secretary can also be pleasant and courteous to teachers, realizing they work under a great deal of pressure at times; therefore, try to get their messages to them and not interrupt the class too much.

21

VALUE-RELATED TESTS

The following instruments provide a means for assessing the self-image of an individual or group to facilitate teaching and counseling toward more responsible behavior.

Each of the instruments utilizes a set of eight value categories: *Affection, Respect, Rectitude/Responsibility, Power/Influence, Skill, Enlightenment, Wealth and Well-Being*. These, according to Dr. Harold D. Lasswell of Yale University, encompass the needs and wants of every individual, no matter what the society or culture.

All of the instruments are available from Pennant Educational Materials.

SIMPSON Perception of Values Inventory (PVI)

The PVI combines both sociometric and personality data in a holistic framework of values. The data is gathered in terms of underlying values rather than in terms of attitude or behavior. Data regarding the value categories can be isolated or combined as desired, since each category is readily identifiable.

The PVI is based upon two premises. First, that the way a person sees himself, the way he sees others, and the way he perceives that others see him, constitutes three major dimensions of personality which influence his attitudes, desires and actions. And second, that these three dimensions are so interrelated that failure to recognize any one dimension severely limits a full analysis of personality.

The PVI is designed for use with groups in grades 4 through adult and can be administered in approximately 30 minutes. Instructions for manual tabulation and analysis are given in the manual. Computer data processing and professional analysis are available from Pennant Educational Materials.

GARDNER Anaylsis of Personality Survey (GAP)

Developed by Dr. Lawrence E. Gardner, the survey provides a graphic representation of how the person responds to a particular set of situations at the time of the survey. His responses provide insight into the hierarchy of values that are of importance to the respondent at that particular time, thereby helping to understand his personality.

Importance is attached to the hierarchy of values as the personality of an individual is the dynamic combination of characteristics, both physical and psychological that make up his identity. These characteristics have their bases in the set of values that the person identifies for himself.

Of particular significance is the fact that the score for each of the eight values is independent of each other and each of the eight value categories is independently evaluated. This makes it possible to make specific judgements as well as to develop behavioral alternatives when using the survey to assist individuals, classes, or schools.

The GAP survey is not a timed instrument but the average individual will take about thirty minutes to complete it. The survey can be scored easily by the administrator in a minimum amount of time. The results give eight separate scores (one for each value analyzed) which may be profiled on a graph. For Grades 7 thru Adult.

MURPHY Inventory of Values (MIV)

Developed by Dr. Maribeth L. Murphy, the inventory is a projective instrument designed for use by guidance counselors, school psychologists, classroom teachers, and persons in the related professions of psychiatry, therapy, and social work.

The MIV is scored objectively to yield a value profile for each subject. The value profile indicates the degree to which the subject's needs are being met, according to his own feeling — realistic or unrealistic.

Diagnostic assessments gained from the MIV are at the level of the subject's own feeling, providing the teacher or therapist with appropriate information around which to develop truly constructive teaching or counseling. He can be more effective in bringing about recognition of the needs of others to improve inter-personal relationships, and he can provide the subject with a basis for responsibility in decision-making.

221

As a group inventory, the MIV may be administered in the classroom to students of grade four and higher. It is adaptable to language arts as a creative writing instrument, and it is useful in social studies, as a point of departure for discussion. As an individual inventory tool, the MIV may be administered to elicit either written or oral responses. For exceptional children, the MIV may be administered to dyslexic, emotionally disturbed, or retarded individuals who are able to dictate their responses to the examiner or to dictation equipment.

The MIV, while primarily useful with children from kindergarten through grade eight, because of the projective nature of the instrument, has been utilized successfully with older students and adults.

SANFORD-SEIDERS Values Inventory of Behavioral Responses (VIBR)

Developed by Dr. Edward W. Sanford, Jr. and Dr. Nancy D. Seiders, the inventory is constructed and designed specifically to measure values within the context of the Lasswell value framework and to show the current status in each value category of individuals and groups of upper-elementary school-age children. The VIBR consists of forty-eight familiar situations in which four alternative choices are provided.

The VIBR is easily scored and can be administered to an individual or class within one sitting, or approximately one hour. The value profile obtained for individuals will reveal areas of deprivation and enhancement, or those areas in which remediation or recognition is needed. After remediation, value shifts can be noted through a second administering of this inventory.

For grades 4, 5 and 6.

22

BOOKS FOR VALUE ANALYSIS
BY CHILDREN

This list is just a beginning. Its real value will be in the additions individual teachers would find suitable for meeting particular needs, interests, grade levels, etc.

Although each selection has been placed in only one area, many are suitable for more than one. Some categories can be filled more easily than others.

AFFECTION

Primary:
> Grandfather & I, Galdone (Lothrop, 1961).
> A Time for Flowers, Taylor (Golden Gate, 1967).
> Amigo. Schweitzer (Macmillan, 1963).

Intermediate:
> Sounder, Armstrong (Har-Row, 1969).
> Onion John, Krumgold (Crowell, 1959).
> The House of Sixty Fathers, De Jong (Harper, 1956).

RESPECT

Primary:
>Crow Boy, Taro Yashima (Viking Press, 1959).
>Play With Me, Ets (Viking Press, 1955).
>Rra-ah, Keith (Bradbury Press, 1969).

Intermediate:
>Sink It Rusty, Christopher (Little, 1963).
>The Cay, Taylor (Doubleday, 1969).
>Viking Adventure, Bulla (Crowell, 1963).

WELL-BEING

Primary:
>If I Were, Hazen (Western, 1970).
>Andy's Happy Day, Reit (Western, 1970).
>The Snowy Day, Keats (Viking, 1962).

Intermediate:
>All of a Kind Family, Taylor (Follett, 1951).
>Little House in the Big Woods (and Series) Wilder (Harper, 1953).
>The Moffats, Estes (Harcourt, 1941).

INFLUENCE

Primary:
>Peggy's New Brother, Schick (Macmillan, 1970).
>Lentil, McCloskey (Viking, 1940).
>Paul, the Hero of the Fire, Ardizzone (E. M. Hale, 1967).

Intermediate:
>In The Year of the Raccoon, Kingman (Houghton, 1966).
>Today I Am a Ham, Parkinson (Abingdon Press, 1968).
>Amos Fortune, Free Man, Yates (E. P. Dutton, 1950).

ENLIGHTENMENT

Primary:
>Two Is a Team, Beim (Harcourt, 1945).
>Sam, Bangs, and Moonshine, Ness (Holt, 1966).
>Time of Wonder, McCloskey (Viking, 1957).

Intermediate:
>Let the Balloon Go, Southall (St. Martin, 1968).
>The Boy Who Wouldn't Talk, Bouchard (Doubleday, 1969).
>D. J's Worst Enemy, Burch (Viking, 1965).

SKILL

Primary:
> Tim and the Tool Chest, Beim (William Morrow, 1951).
> Blaze Shows the Way, Anderson (Macmillan, 1969).
> Timothy Robbins Climbs the Mountain, Tressett (E. M. Hale, 1960).

Intermediate:
> Follow My Leader, Garfield (Viking, 1957).
> Henry 3, Krumgold (Altaneum, 1967).
> Sound of Sunshine, Sound of Rain, Heide (Parents, 1970).

WEALTH

Primary:
> Umbrella, Yashima (Viking, 1958).
> No Room for Freddy, Reit (Western, 1970).
> Two Pesos for Catalina, Kein (E. M. Hall, 1960).

Intermediate:
> Henry Reed's Babysitting Service, Robertson (Viking, 1966).
> Cotton in My Sack, Lenski (Lippincott, 1949).
> The Janitor's Girl, Friedman (Morros, 1952).

RESPONSIBILITY

Primary:
> Have You Seen Louie? Munro (Western, 1970).
> Tim to the Lighthouse, Ardizzone (Henry Z. Walck, 1968).
> One Horse Farm, Ipcar (Doubleday, 1950).

Intermediate:
> Across Five Aprils, Hunt (Follett, 1964).
> The White Archer, an Eskimo Legend, Houston (Harcourt, 1967).
> The Street of the Flower Boxes, Mann (Coward, 1966).

23

VALUE-RELATED RESEARCH

For further reading on research related to the Lasswell value framework, the following dissertations are suggested.

All are available for review at U.S. International University, 8655 Pomerado Road, San Diego, California 92124.

Abstracts and copies are available through University Microfilms, Ann Arbor, Michigan.

Abrams, Macy L. & Saxon, James A.

VIDAC: A Computer Program for Value Identification and Classification

Ph.D. diss. USIU 1968 (Univ. Micro. #17-1236)

A comprehensive system for studying and evaluating student values through computerized study of the words used by students. Expands Lasswell's earlier "dictionary". Can be used in any district that has or can secure data-processing services.

BECOMING AWARE OF VALUES

Bensley, Marvin Leroy

Values Enhancement for Children through Non-Directive Inservice Teacher Training

Ph.D. diss. USIU 1970 (Univ. Micro. 70-22347)

Evaluation of an experiment in nondirective training at several elementary grade levels in one Southern California school district (Coronado). Indicates significant results.

Gardner, Lawrence Edward

Effects of Community College Education on Students' Concepts of their Value Goals

Ph.D. diss. USIU 1969 (Univ. Micro. 70-12538)

Has important relevancy to high school teachers particularly, although elementary teachers may well see "roots" in the grades.

Giles, Joseph R.

Significant Teenage Value Conflicts: Their Perception of the Parents' Values versus Their Parents' Perception of Teenagers' Values

M.A. Thesis USIU 1968 (not microfilmed)

An excellent start for a teacher-parent discussion dialog (or parent-student dialog).

Higgins, Elizabeth Barkman

An Exploratory Investigation of the Valuing Process of Some Fourth Grade Pupils

Ph.D. diss. 1968 (Univ. Micro. 69-19825)

This is an excellent description of the application of the valuing techniques by one teacher in one grade level. The results are convincing and have been subsequently supported by replicated study.

Kerby, John Blue

Case-Study Analysis of the Development of a Prototype for Comprehensive Education in Human Values

Ph.D. diss. USIU 1968 (no micro. number available)

Highly recommended for those who want the basic concepts behind the values teaching program.

228

Kutcher, Ernest Leo

The Relationship between the Use of the Human Values Series Readers and Reading Comprehension

Ph.D. diss. USIU 1969 (no micro. number)

A basic study of the actual use of the Rucker, et al. textbooks on valuing for elementary grades.

Murphy, Maribeth Logan

Measurement of Values Through Responses to Selected Visual Stimulus Materials

Ph.D. diss. USIU 1970 (Univ. Micro. 70-11416)

This research study lays the background for the development, piloting and use of the Murphy measurement instrument now used in a number of districts and states.

Phelps, Jimmy Frances

Analysis of an Inservice Program in Human Values Education

Ph.D. diss. USIU 1971 (no micro number yet available)

Miss Phelps is the highly successful curriculum director for the Santee School District and has been in the forefront of the experiment and expansion of the valuing program in that district. She has conducted the teacher training programs at Santee and may be considered an "authority" on the program and its results to date.

Sanford, Jr., Edward W. & Seiders, N. D.

Change in Value Status of Elementary School Children after Instruction in a Values-Oriented Rationale

Ph.D. diss. USIU   1969 (Univ. Micro. #70-9804)

This is the basis for the Sanford-Seiders attitude measuring manual and system. It is basic to a study of the teaching potentials of the values strategy.

Skidmore, Charles Ernest

Analysis of a Model for Implementing Value Learning in a School District

Ph.D. diss. USIU 1970 (Univ. Micro. #70-22336)

This is a longitudinal report by the superintendent of the Santee School District, Santee, California.

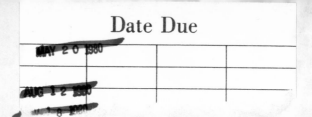